When War Follows You Home

Published in 2023 by Welford Publishing

ISBN: Paperback 978-1-7390970-0-4

A catalogue for this book is available from the British Library.

Editor Christine McPherson

When War Follows You Home

Ben Close

I want to dedicate this first book to my hero and rock my grandad G. Alan Close, 26/6/1936.

I hope I haven't disappointed you and I have made you proud.

Secondly, I would like to dedicate this book to all personnel who have paid the ultimate sacrifice or who continue to suffer from serving in all of the OPTELIC and Bosnia tours.

Contents

How Do You Say Goodbye?

Have you ever had to say goodbye to someone that you love with all your heart, knowing that you'll never see them again? How do you find those final words? How do you find the strength to walk away, when your entire body wants to collapse on the spot and never leave? How do you pick up the pieces of your life to keep living, when it feels like part of you also died that day?

I will never forget the day in the year 2000 when I was told that my grandad, my hero in my life, had cancer. It was terminal, and I was devastated. I visited him a lot while he was poorly, and although I struggled with my emotions, I just had to see him. It also broke my heart seeing how much it hurt my nan; she was the love of his life.

They had both always been a big part of my life. When I was younger, they took me away on holidays, and for days out in the summer to theme parks and swimming. Most years, they took me on holiday to Spain, and twice we went to Florida, making up for me having an absent father at the time. It was my grandad who took me to my very first football match – Luton vs Manchester United.

Every time I visited them in Luton, we would go to the local Sea Cadet Centre based there. Grandad had all the keys, because he oversaw the security of the centre and its grounds. I always took my air rifle along, and he and I would go rat shooting, or out on a boat. Even if he was just cleaning the place up, I loved to help him. Like I said, he was my hero, and would always tell me stories about his time in the Army.

Before he retired, he had been a senior manager at Vauxhall, as a mechanic. As I got older, if I was in Luton on a Saturday night, I'd go with Nan and Grandad to the local working men's club to listen to some music and have a few beers. I loved him and my nan so much, and even when I started going out with friends and had girlfriends, I always made time to visit them in Luton.

I will never forget the last time I saw him. He was lying in bed in his home, literally hanging by a thread, and as I walked into the bedroom, he saw me and stretched out his arms. I gave him a huge cuddle and didn't want to let go of him. I was trying so hard not to cry in front of him. My mum, standing by my side, was also trying not to cry, but she couldn't hold it in.

I could see tears in Grandad's eyes; he knew this would be our last cuddle… and so did I. With a huge lump in my throat, I somehow found the words to say goodbye to my hero and promised that I would make him proud by becoming a soldier. I put my thumb up to him and he did the same, then I left the room with my mum, both of us in floods of tears.

When he took his final breath, my whole world collapsed. I didn't know how I would cope, but I knew that no matter what happened in my life, I had to keep my promise.

Chapter 1

The Army Dream Began

I was in the Army Cadet Force (ACF) from the age of 12, mainly because it helped me to feel safe at night. Whilst most kids kept football cards and the occasional dodgy magazine under their bed, I had a baseball bat and a set of knives underneath mine. I had learnt from an early age that there are some people in life you can't trust. Not only did I have to protect myself, but I needed to take care of my mum and my younger brother and sister.

The ACF is a great organisation; it keeps kids off the streets and teaches some form of discipline and respect. It's not the Army, but you still wear uniform, learn basic drill, weapon training, and field craft. And as time progresses, you go through the training syllabus and rank structure, and that's when it becomes more like the Army, including longer training like their Ranger course, which I did when I was 15. As you are still a child, there are of course limits on what you can do and be taught at ACF. But every year there would be an annual camp held at an Army training area, were you would stay for one week, live in Army accommodation, and take part in various activities. These included a military-style 24-hour tactical exercise, as well as rock climbing and cannoning. It's a good organisation for kids to be part of, and some of the adult instructors were ex-soldiers. I met many good friends with the ACF, and am still mates with some of them today.

By the time I was 15, I knew I wanted to join the Army and become an infantry soldier. In the last few years of school, I had been diagnosed with Dyslexia and Dyscalculia, and although I thankfully didn't have to go to the special needs department, I was entitled to extra help and more time for exams. However, as a young teenager, the last thing you want is to bring any kind of attention to yourself, and all I wanted to do was fit in. For me, acting the clown seemed to be the better option.

The only subject I really enjoyed and was good at was PE. I was a keen footballer and liked to box, but school didn't allow us to box, so we did it in the woods instead or after school. My gran was the head English teacher at the local girls' school a short distance from my school, and me and the boys would regularly skip a class so we could be at the girls' school around lunch time. Unfortunately, we usually got caught because the girls would talk, and of course my gran would find out then tell my mum. And as Mum was an Education Welfare Officer, that really didn't go down well!

By that time, I was going off the rails a little, and I remember going to France for an 'educational' trip, but me and a few mates found a little bar and spent the day drinking beer. The teachers must have known we were pissed, because my mum knew all about it the minute I walked through the door.

Towards the end of Year 10, I was regularly in the headmaster's office on a report card, and several times I was suspended. Finally, I was offered a placement at Moulton College with a group of other lads, doing bricklaying, woodwork, cooking, and estate management. It meant that I would get an NVQ in those subjects but would have to drop a lot of GCSEs – something that didn't bother me at all. So, I accepted the placement.

While I was in the last year of school, my friend Martin and I managed to get fake IDs that said we were 18 years old, which meant we could go and buy alcohol and go to pubs. Sometimes we even got drunk before school or at lunch time. One afternoon, Martin and I took a few girls home to my house, and we bought a bottle of vodka and cans of beer. We all went back to school shit-faced, and one of the girls passed out in the carpark. A doctor was sent for, and her parents were called to pick her up.

One Thursday, Martin and I hit a nightclub in town, and drove home pissed on his 50cc motor bike. The next day at school I felt like pure shit, and one of the teachers asked me, "Ben, did you have a good night at Club XS?"

I asked innocently, "Sir, what are you on about?"

But he just laughed and replied, "Ben, I was there, and you were telling me and another teacher how much you hated some of the teachers!"

I felt sick, but he just winked at me and walked past.

Unsurprisingly, I didn't do very well in my GCSEs. But I wasn't bothered, because I knew what I wanted to do – to be a combat soldier and fight for my country. So, as soon as I turned 16, I went to my local Army Careers Office and completed the relevant paperwork.

Chapter 2
Army Selection

2002, 17 years old

Once I had completed my first interview and my barb test – the initial computer test to see what you could do within the Army – I was sent to the Lichfield Selection Centre. That next stage, which lasted two days, involved a medical examination, fitness tests, and then a final interview. I was issued with a train warrant to get me there, and I was so excited to start my journey as a soldier.

When I arrived, we had a team welcome briefing, followed by the medical. Everything was going well, and the nurse was going through my medical history when she brought up the fact that I had been given an inhaler when I was 10 years old, for one month, due to a chest infection. Before I could say another word, she had stamped my paperwork and told me I would not be able to continue with Army selection, and to come back in a minimum of two years.

My dream had been shattered, and I had to get the train back home the same day. I was totally gutted. Joining the Army was all I had ever wanted to do, and I'd been so confident when I'd told all my friends I was going for selection. Worse than that, I felt like I had let down my grandad, because I had promised him that I was going to be a soldier before he passed away.

I went home and felt like a total waste of space. In all honesty, I let myself go for a month or two, out drinking in the pubs and getting into fights in town. I just didn't give a shit at that point.

Mum suggested I go to college and do public services, and if I still wanted to join the Army when I was 18, she would support me by writing a letter of appeal. I wasn't over excited about going back to college, as I'd hated school and expected just more of the same. But I went along with it, and also managed to get a part-time job at a fast-food restaurant. That provided me with the cash I needed so I could go out with friends drinking and chasing girls, but I absolutely hated the job.

College was okay, and I enjoyed most topics on public services, apart from the key skills modules. So, I would regularly skip those classes and sit in the local pub. My favourite subjects were PT (physical training), where we did boxing and self-defence tactics. We also went out on orienteering trips, which were good.

During the holidays I would work full time at the fast-food restaurant, and even though I hated it, I liked having the money to do what I wanted.

My public services course only lasted one year, so then I enrolled in the Prince's Trust Award Scheme, which was more hands-on, doing projects and learning good skills for life. I smashed that course, even though I turned up pissed some days and got sent home. In my defence, it was during the World Cup and the pubs in town were open from 6am!

After I had completed my courses, I didn't have a lot to concentrate on, and I still had the best part of eight months to wait before I could re-apply for the Army. So I began working full time at the restaurant, but was really fed up there. I just wanted to be a soldier.

I started to go out on a Thursday, Friday, and Saturday, getting plastered and into fights with grown men. A few of these fights were nasty, with people getting seriously hurt and arrested. I was only arrested once at that point, and got away with it with no further action. I thought I would never get caught and have to deal with the consequences, but was proved wrong later in life…

Often, I would turn up to work at the restaurant still pissed, and kept getting in trouble for it. Once I went out on a Friday night with friends to Club XS, where it was £10 entry and drinks were free all night. On the Saturday morning, I started work at 6am for the breakfast shift. I don't remember much, but I was woken up by the duty manager in the doorway of my job, still pissed! I was sent home by 10am, unfit for work. I went back in there that evening for food, drunk again, and I even had the cheek to ring in sick the next day. I received a written warning for that.

My mate Gezz, who is still a friend today, had an employment agency, so I went to see him and he found me full time work in warehouses with my best friend Jay. The pay was better, so I never went back to the fast-food restaurant except to eat.

Chapter 3
Territorial Army Selection

As I was bored waiting for the regular Army, I decided I would try my luck at the local Territorial Army Centre in Corby – 118 Recovery Company (REME). I went along on a parade night, filled out all the relevant paperwork, and was then sent to a GP in Northampton for a medical. I didn't mention that I had failed an Army medical 18 months before, and this time I passed and was put on the next selection weekend, which was only two weeks away.

The selection weekend was based at 116 Recovery Company in Northampton, where we did a fitness test, walking and running around a park with a weighted bergen (rucksack), which is also known as tabbing. We also did team building exercises, and finished the weekend with a night-time exercise at Yardley Chase training area. It was pissing down with rain, but at least it only lasted about 12 hours.

After this, we all got changed into smart clothes for an interview with the Company Commander, and he went through our results individually. I was happy to learn that I had passed and was accepted into 118 Recovery Company. This meant I would be given an Army number and start being paid as a trainee craftsman for parade nights and weekends away. From then on, I went every Tuesday night and any weekend that came up, as I was really keen to learn.

I began working on my fitness with a guy called Garry, who lived near my mum. He was a serving infantry soldier – a Colour Sergeant. I wanted to make sure my fitness was at a high standard, that I could tab with weight and run at least a mile-and-a-half in under ten minutes.

My only problem was that I was with the REME, but I really wanted to be a combat soldier. I started to look into joining the French Foreign Legion, liked what I saw, and was prepared to go to Marseille to join up. But Mum didn't want me to join the Legion, and I don't blame her. I was too young really, but I just wanted to be a proper soldier, not a weekend warrior.

So, on my eighteenth birthday, the first thing I did was ask Mum to send a letter of appeal to the Army so that I could hopefully try again... and keep my promise to my grandad.

Chapter 4
On Her Majesty's Service Letter

Shortly after my birthday, I received a brown letter marked "On Her Majesty's Service". It was a response from the letter of appeal which Mum had sent to the Army, and stated that in order to go back to Lichfield for selection, I would first have to pass a medical at Frimley Park Hospital.

I booked my appointment and, luckily, got in very quickly. There I was asked to take my top off, then they connected me up to a computer and asked me to run on the treadmill for ten minutes. I was pretty fit anyway, so this was no problem. Afterwards, a doctor checked my breathing and listened to my chest and lungs, then sent me to sit in the waiting room. After a short time I was called into the office for my results. I'd passed! I was so excited, because this meant I could now go back and apply for selection.

The next day I was down at the Army Recruitment Office armed with all my paperwork. The Recruitment Sergeant was Lee from the Guards, and he spoke to me about the history of his regiment and said that if I chose them, he would get me on the next selection, which was only one week away. I jumped at the chance and walked out of the office with my rail warrant to go back for selection in less than a week's time.

Lee had also given me a booklet on the Guards, which I read through time and time again. I was still nervous about the medical at selection, in case they came up with a load of new bullshit to stop me joining, but any thought of joining the French Foreign Legion had completely left my head. My full focus was on the Guards.

Chapter 5
Army Selection, Round Two

It was the morning of my selection, and I had to get the 0600 hours train from Kettering in order to be on time, as it involved a few stops and changes before Lichfield. I felt sick on the journey – a mixture of hunger and nerves – and I just didn't know how I would react if I faced rejection again.

I got to Lichfield train station at around 9am to find a soldier with a blue clipboard taking down names, and a big white bus waiting – just like the last time when I had been there two years before.

When we got to the selection centre, it was the same format – a brief, then the medical – and I recognised most of the instructors from the previous time. I went for my medical, but this time I was armed with all my paperwork, just in case. Thankfully, this time I passed the medical and was able to continue with the selection process, but then I started worrying that I wasn't fit enough or that I might fail a team building exercise.

The next day we did strength exercises, team building, and the dreaded bleep test. I was exhausted by the end of the day, and I had no idea if I had passed, because you don't get your results till the end of selection the following day. That evening, we went to the on-site bar, known as the NAAFI, for a couple of hours to relax and chat to some of the others on selection. Then it was bedtime, so we walked in a group to the accommodation. I was fucked, so pretty much got my head down straight away.

Reveille (wake up) was at 05.30, and breakfast served at 6am. We then went back to the accommodation to clean up and hand in our bed sheets.

Next, we had our Personal Fitness Test (PFT). This involved a 1.5 mile run around camp in two groups, but everyone was running to record their own personal best time. For the infantry, you had to complete the run in less than 10.3 minutes.

We had to go round the course first with a Physical Training Instructor (PTI), jogging at a slow pace and walking the 1.5-mile route. Once that was completed, the PFT began. I ran my heart out around the course and tried so hard that when I crossed the finish line, I was physically sick. Once the run was completed, we couldn't lie down or sit, but had to stand with our hands behind our backs in three ranks, one behind the other. I worked out that I must have finished in the top six out of about 30 people, but I wasn't sure.

Once everyone had finished, we went back to the accommodation for a shower and to change into our best clothes for our final interview and the results of selection. We all sat nervously in the briefing room, waiting for our names to be called. If you came out with a certificate, it meant you had a job; if not, it meant that you had failed somewhere on selection and would have to try again. The ratio seemed to be about three-in-five coming out with a job.

I remember when my name was called, I was shaking and felt like I had just run ten miles. I couldn't get my breath. Then I walked in and sat down in front of the Major. Even if I had passed all my tests, it would still be his final decision whether or not I got through. He waffled on for about ten minutes before telling me my results. I had passed every test and completed my 1.5 mile run in 9.25 minutes. He then asked me a few more questions before handing me a certificate and shaking my hand.

Finally, I had passed and been accepted to go on the Guards training, based at the Infantry Training Centre (IRTC) in Catterick.

I rang Mum straight away, and she was so pleased for me. I then rang the Recruitment Sergeant Lee, who told me to go into the office on the Monday so that I could swear my allegiance to the Queen and sign the Official Secrets Act. I celebrated that weekend – making sure I stayed out of trouble – and on the Monday took the oath and signed all the official paperwork. I was told the next intake was on the 13th of October, which was only six weeks away.

I couldn't believe I was finally going to join the Army in just six weeks!

I handed in my notice to the employment agency and started to prepare for my six months of Guards Infantry training. I knew it was going to be hard work and a big challenge, because the Guards didn't just accept anyone; you had to be the best in order to pass out and join your Battalion.

Chapter 6
Phase One –
Basic Training

13th October, 2003

Mum insisted she wanted to drive me to Catterick, even though it was a four-hour journey from Kettering. We left at 6am on the Monday morning, and on the way there I had mixed emotions of excitement and nerves.

We arrived just before lunchtime, and I said my goodbyes, watching Mum leave in tears. It would be four weeks until we saw our families again, although we could call them on a pay-phone. Mobiles were not to be used, and were locked away.

I was at Helles Barracks, which was old and falling apart. We shared our block with the recruits from the Parachute Regiment, while across the road in the new block were the Ghurkhas. Our regiment and the Paras used the same Mess Hall (where we ate) and the Ghurkhas had their own, but we all shared the NAAFI.

On arrival, we met our Section Commanders. Mine was a very angry Scottish Sergeant from a Guards Regiment. (To-day we are friends, but at the time we were not. He had a job to do, though!) We had to hand in all mobile phones, stereos, and anything that was not military issue, other than photos of family. We were then given regimental tracksuits to put on, and all our civilian clothes went into our soldier boxes, which were locked with a padlock and placed under the bed.

For the first six weeks we were not allowed to leave camp at all, unless on exercise with a PTI or a Section Commander. We could not drink alcohol in the NAAFI either. This is another difference between the Guards and regular infantry training. They were allowed to drink after work on a two-can rule, and to leave camp as long as they returned by a certain time.

After haircuts – number ones all round with clippers – we were put into three ranks and marched to the clothing stores to get our military uniforms and equipment, then marched back. By the time we returned, there were sheets and itchy, prison-style blankets ready to be set up on each bed.

It was then time for lesson one: how to wash, and brush your teeth! A Sergeant was naked in the shower demonstrating how to wash, shave, and brush your teeth at the same time. I thought it was a load of bollocks, but I was surprised how many people had such poor hygiene.

After this lesson, we went for a tour of the whole camp. There was another barracks through the tunnel, which is where the gym was based. It was one mile from our block, and we had to run or march there. As we got through the tunnel, one of the Sergeants shouted that this was where regular infantry potential soldiers trained. We called them Chippies. (Chippy means an infantry soldier from a regular unit, not a Guards unit, and their training is somewhat different. They have a name for us as well.)

Over the first few days, we were shown the basics of foot drill. And for the first six weeks, we had to call out the timings of the drill movements, shouting "LEFT, RIGHT, LEFT, RIGHT", depending on which boot hit the floor. When we halted, we would shout "HALT CHECK, ONE, TWO. "There are so many words of command it would take me all day to explain, but that was the basics.

During our entire six months of training, we had to march everywhere around camp, whether we were on our own going to the NAAFI or in a group; it didn't matter. If we were seen not marching, we would be pushed physically and mentally beyond all of our barriers, which was known as beasting. I didn't mind beasting; for me, the physically harder it was, the better.

The first couple of days were quite boring, as we had to sit through a lot of "death by PowerPoint" presentations, and were taught how to look presentable by ironing our clothes and polishing our boots properly, how our lockers must look at all times, and that our beds must be made every morning by 06.00.

After all the briefs were done we got down to real training. Those first weeks (phase 1) is the time when they basically beat you down from being a civilian to a soldier, and teach you the basics. During that initial six weeks, we were told we would have to pass a number of tests, such as Skill at Arms with the SA80, which is the personal weapon system used by any soldier. In training, we had the old-style SA80s – the A1, which was shit because it always jammed when firing and would rust after an hour in the rain, so needed lots of cleaning. The SA80 A2 had not long been introduced, so only the Operational Battalions had them. On the whole, all the drills were the same, just some used a better rifle.

We also had to do a basic shooting test with live ammunition; had room and locker inspections (every day); and underwent fitness tests, including a loaded march with weight and weapon (TAB). This all led up to the Adjutant's room and locker inspection, followed by the six-week pass-out test. Should you not pass this, your weekend would be cancelled, and the test would have to be repeated.

A normal day would consist of 0530 reveille, we would then have a wash and shave and give our block a clean (known as swabbing) before 0630. Then we would all get in three ranks and march to the cook house for breakfast. We had about 30 minutes to eat before marching back to the block, where we would all then do some more swabbing and make sure our lockers were in good order for our daily room and locker inspection by the Section Commanders. We hardly ever passed the inspection, so the kit in the locker would go out the window.

I came to the decision early on to sleep in my sleeping bag on the floor with my roll mat, as I had made my bed perfectly and that way I wouldn't need to make it each morning – saving me ten minutes. I got away with this for a while, until one morning we had a surprise wake-up call with a Sergeant and Willy the Whistle. He spotted me on the floor in my fart sack, so my bed and all the sheets were tossed out the window!

By 0800, we had to be outside in three ranks for our daily inspection – and again, we rarely passed. Anyone who failed would be placed on a show clean parade at 2200 hours outside the guard room, where a duty officer from either the Guards or Parachute Regiment would re-inspect you. If you failed that, you would be back there at 0600 hours the following morning and placed on report. Being on parade meant you would find yourself with extra duties or extra show parades, which is shit.

After all the daily inspections were over, we took part in infantry training. It was never the same, but for the first six weeks it was basic soldier skills, and we would do PT every day. We learnt things like skill at arms with SA80; basic foot drill; field craft; shooting live ammunition on the range; PT; and map reading. We were also deployed for a couple of exercises in the field. One lasted a full night; another was three nights' long and tactical. We learnt how to live and keep hygiene up when in the field, along with basics like section attacks, patrolling, and how to fight using blank ammunition, smoke grenades, and flash bangs. It was good infantry training, and I loved all aspects of it.

After three weeks, we were given our drill boots, which were big heavy boots with studs on the bottom to give more of an effect when doing drill. These have to be filled with sand covered in beeswax, then a blow torch is used to melt the beeswax onto the boots for shining purposes. Everyone suffered bad blisters for a week or two of wearing in the boots; mine were so bad that I was allowed to wear my military trainers for two days to allow the blisters to go down.

From the moment we had the drill boots beeswaxed, we would have a shiny parade every night from 1830 till 2000. That involved us all sitting in the corridor with our regimental tracksuits on, with a tin of polish and selvyt cloth, buffing our drill boots to get them to the Guards' standard for royal duties. All we could talk about in that time was regimental history. This shiny parade went on throughout the whole of basic training if we were not in the field.

Chapter 7
Week Four – Parents' Day

10th November

On week four we had an open day when parents could come and see the progress their sons had made. We had a number of stands for them to walk round, which showed everything we had done up until this point. They walked around our rooms, saw our lockers, and the guys who had picked up foot drill the best put on a marching parade for them.

I was on the camouflage and concealment stand, which was being run by my Sergeant. There were four of us in the woods, all spread out, and the Sergeant was talking to the visitors about how and why things are seen. Two of the guys were easy to spot, then there was a guy deeper in the woods who could be seen when pointed out. Then he told everyone that there was one more soldier to find – that was me. I did the stand five times throughout the day, and not one person saw me until I stood up. I was lying down just ten metres from them, with a cam cream sniper's ghillie suit on and a rifle. The crowd were amazed when I stood up.

After the stands had been visited, food was available, and we could all go and join our families in the NAAFI. The drinking ban was also lifted for the day. I had my mum there, along with my dad, brother, sister, and gran, and it was nice to see them all.

While in the NAAFI, our Platoon Sergeant announced that we could get a pass and leave camp if we were with our families, but we had to be back by midnight. My mum, gran, and siblings had to go home, but Dad had booked a hotel room close by, so he and I went out and got drunk in Richmond. It was a good night, but I couldn't get a taxi and I was late, so Dad – pissed – drove me back to camp in the early hours of the morning. Nothing was said, but I think that's because everyone was pissed that night.

The next morning was Remembrance Day, and we had a parade on the drill square at 11am. I felt very shaky and ill, probably because it was the first time I had been drinking in four weeks. When the Padre asked us to pray, I am ashamed to say that I fainted, had to be dragged off the drill square, and was taken to the medical centre. It was the first time I had fainted in my life, but luckily the Medical Officer knew it had been Parents' Day the day before, so he cut me some slack and nothing more was said.

Chapter 8

Adjutant's Six-Week Pass-Off Parade

After six weeks we had a full inspection from the Adjutant, which consisted of room and locker inspections, asking us questions about regimental history while we were standing to attention next to our beds, then an inspection on the drill square, followed by a marching parade. If he was happy with us, we could sign for some money and go home for a long weekend. This would mean that phase one was over and we could stop shouting out all the timings when doing foot drill.

We seemed to do okay on the parade – you could never get it perfect! – as we passed and were allowed to go home that day (Thursday), but had to be back on Monday by 1800 hours. We all signed out £180 from the Platoon Commander (Officer), along with a rail warrant card to get us home and back. By the time that was done, we had just 20 minutes to get changed into our suits before the bus left for Darlington train station. A few of us on the same train quickly got the beers in, and we were very loud all the way to our stops.

That weekend went really quickly. I got very drunk on the first night, then went out on the Saturday with friends. On the Sunday we had a family meal, and at one point I realised I had become so used to standing to attention that I was doing it in my mum's kitchen!

Monday came, and I headed back to camp, but it was surprising how many people never came back after that first weekend off.

Chapter 9
Phase Two

The next 22 weeks covered our trade training, and as we were Infantry that meant our trade was combat. So, things would now become harder both physically and mentally.

We were introduced to weapons drill at this point, which involved marching with your SA80 and bayonet. Being Guards, we had to be trained for royal duties as well as for war. The standard for drill became a lot harder, as everything had to be perfect every day, and if it wasn't you found yourself at the Guard Room at 2200 hours. I think I spent most of my evenings at the Guard Room.

PT got harder, too. We had to carry heavier kit for longer Tabs and runs, sometimes doing two PT sessions per day, preparing us for our combat fitness test before passing out. We also had a few trips to the local swimming pool where we did the military swimming test. You had to jump in the pool in full kit, including webbing (pouches attached to a yoke so you can carry ammunition/water/medical kit, and 24 hours of rations). We swam around the pool for 20 minutes in full kit, then treaded water for two minutes. It sounds easy, but I can assure you it's not when you are in full kit and wearing boots.

Chapter 10

Christmas Leave

As we were on a winter course, we were given two weeks' leave for Christmas. I went back home to Mum's and really started to feel like a soldier. We were also issued with our MOD 90 (Army ID). Christmas was nice with the family, and it was good fun going out drinking with my friends, but it passed quickly and soon it was time to be back at work.

After the festive break we were all drug tested, and a couple of guys who were caught out were immediately discharged.

At that stage we were allowed to bring our own duvets and pillows, and we could also have a TV in our room if we had one, and a stereo player so that we could listen to music.

All the recruits still in our company at this point had passed weapon handling and basic shooting military tests, so we could do barrack guard with live ammunition (lucky us!). I was fortunate enough to pull quite a lot of night duties. At first it was good to hold a weapon with live ammunition and guard the camp, but the novelty soon wore off.

We were also told that if we worked hard all week, didn't fuck up, and were not on exercise or guard duty, we would be stood down from Friday night till Sunday night. This meant we could go home or out on the piss in Darlington. Even though I had a girlfriend at home, going out on the piss in

Darlington seemed much more appealing for a number of reasons which I'm sure you can guess.

That first week back after the Christmas holidays, we were beasted with PT for a week to get rid of our turkey and beer guts!

The Section Commanders then started introducing us to other weapon systems we would be using, like the GPMG a 7.62 machine gun; the LMG 5.56 machine gun; LSW; the anti-tank weapon (LAW); HE grenades. The most daunting was using live HE grenades – what if I dropped it or something went wrong? – but it was really exciting.

Our exercises in the field grew longer and harder, and we would be tactical from start to finish. The exercises ranged from three nights up to two weeks. As they were completely tactical, there was no light at night or talking, we would all take turns on stag (watch duties) throughout the day and night, and be sent out on all sorts of patrols/operations around the clock. Even though ours was a winter course (from October till April), because we were Guards, we were not allowed to go out and buy any Gucci kit like gas burners and electric shavers, or any warm kit like softy jackets and decent gloves, or have noodles to eat.

All we could use on exercise was what we had been issued by the clothing stores, and all we could eat was the ration packs we had been issued, which we could only heat up with issued Hexi cookers and Hexi blocks lit with issued matches. There was no way round this, because our kit was checked by Section Commanders before and at the end of every exercise, and life wasn't worth living if you got caught out cheating in any way.

It's fair enough really when you look back, because if you can operate with the bare minimum of kit, then you can operate no matter what. But at the time it pissed us off seeing the other regiments cutting around the training area in softies and Gucci kit!

We also did training in fighting in a built-up area (FIBUA), going from house to house, through doors and windows, fighting the enemy. We all loved FIBUA, but it was a fucking lick out. In other words, we were physically and mentally fucked.

We did a lot more live firing with all the weapons we had trained on to prepare for our final shooting tests (APWT). If you passed that, it was on to battle camp for a week of live firing march and shoots, and live fire ranges doing section and platoon attacks near the end of training. If you failed, though, you could not pass out, but were put back into a platoon behind you in training and made to do it all again. We had a fair amount of people who did not meet the requirements and were put back a few weeks. In some cases, people were discharged out of the Army for injury in training, or just not being able to meet the standard needed.

Chapter 11
Tactical Exercise – Trench Digging

We had heard horror stories about this exercise, but for some reason I was quite looking forward to it. It was a five-day exercise, so we had all our normal kit checks and were issued sandbags, pickets of all sizes, shovels, thumpers, pickaxes, razor and barbed wire, and gloves – and, of course, Wriggly Tin (a corrugated metal tin). Then we mounted our designated green Army Bedford truck in sections at 0700 hours. We drove for a good three hours, by which time everybody's arse, back, and legs were hurting from being thrown around in the back.

We arrived at the training area around midday and patrolled up to our Platoon Commander and Platoon Sergeant, roughly a mile away. When we got there, we saw a readymade trench, which they tried to tell us had taken them two hours to make by hand. We knew that was bullshit the minute we started; it was difficult cutting through the rocks and was clearly going to take days rather than hours. We had a lesson on how to build a defence trench then were given our orders. A trench of this size would typically be as deep as the tallest man, with room for a section of eight soldiers.

We had to tab off to a location where the Army transport trucks, known as Bedfords, would be waiting with all the trench-digging equipment. Each section had to dig a defence trench, wearing body armour (CBA) and helmets, and only once the trench was complete could we get into routine – which means rest, staging on, personal admin, and sleep.

The only other time we would be excused from digging was if it was our stag duties, doing an hour in the day, doubling up at night, doing two hours apiece before being relieved, and then it was back to digging. Stagging was probably harder than digging, because we were fucked and started falling asleep, but sleeping was the last thing you wanted to be caught doing or we would all suffer for it. So, we regularly checked on the guys on stag, giving them a kick if they dozed off.

At one point, the Section Commander saw me dozing off while digging, so he hit me with a shovel over my head. Good job I was wearing my helmet, but it certainly woke me up straight away!

First, after marking off where the trench is going to be, you have to de-turf the grass. Then the real fun starts. I never expected it to be so difficult, but there was solid rock under the soil, so we had to use pickaxes and thumpers with six-foot pickets.

By sundown on the first night, it looked like we had barely started, so we carried on digging throughout the night, in the rain, only stopping for a hot brew and some food.

It's weird how we all felt fucked during the night, but when the sun came up on day two, it seemed to wake us up. Well, it did for me. We stopped for breakfast, which was sausage and beans in a boil-in-the-bag or, if we were lucky, corned beef hash. Then it was back to digging.

Section Commanders regularly came round checking us and kicking off that it should be done quicker. All the rock we broke up when digging was put into sandbags so that we could build up the defence around the trench when we'd finished.

By sundown on the second night, we were still not finished, and we all felt what tired really meant. Men were dropping like flies, falling asleep standing up and hallucinating. Lots of guys were taken off the exercise by the medic – I think to rest – but this then made it harder for the rest of us.

Day three, I was fucked. It was the longest I had ever gone without sleep; it was probably the same for everyone else. However, we carried on. Everyone had blisters all over their hands and we were all shattered, but we were finally starting to see an end result. That day was by far the hardest. I was falling asleep standing up, and I felt like I had been drinking non-stop for three days.

That night I started hallucinating as if I had been on acid at a rave. I remember seeing a big building with a swimming pool. I started walking towards it, but really I was walking into the woods. Luckily, one of the Section Commanders spotted me. I remember him touching me, and when I turned round he looked like an alien. I could see a big beard growing off his head and chin (clearly, it wasn't really there). He gave me some chocolate and some coffee then walked me back to my trench. It was raining at the time, and the raindrops looked multi-coloured to me, bouncing off the floor – like I said, as if I was on acid at a rave.

We had all finished the trenches by the morning of the fourth day and were told we could stand down and sleep in our sleeping bags. My boots came straight off, and I was out immediately.

We woke up to shouting and gunfire four hours later! Clearly, it was a plan that we were being attacked by the enemy and had to bug out of our positions. We packed our kit, still half asleep and disorientated, trying to fire back. I could not find my boots and I was shouting, "Where the fuck are my boots?" In the end, I had to bug out through the mud in my socks.

Once we bugged out, we all received a major bollocking for not being quick enough. The Section Commander shouted, "You weasels aren't good enough for the Guards. You are all getting fucked off to those Chippy fuckers. You are shit!" Of course, this was all a game. I know that now, but at the time it was soul destroying. I then had my boots thrown at me.

The next phase of the exercise was a dawn attack the following morning, when we had to fight and win our trench positions back. We had a rest before this to feel as fresh as possible, then we deployed to the line of departure and waited to attack.

We never fucked up, and although the attack was hard, it seemed to go well. During the reorganisation (REORG) after the attack, my Section Commander had a disagreement with another Section Commander, and it ended up in a full-blown fight. We were all killing ourselves laughing, and the fight only ended when another Sergeant went over and broke it up.

Once the end of the exercise was called, we had the joy of taking down all defences, re-filling the trenches, then finally returfing the grass, which took hours and was shit. It was a Friday, and we all wanted to get back and get out on the piss for the weekend.

So, training continued to get more advanced, and PT was getting longer, but we were getting fitter at the same time.

Chapter 12

Bayonet Assault – Course One

We all looked forward to bayonet training, as we knew it would be hard but fun at the same time. We were wakened at 0500 and told we had a room and locker inspection. It was snowing, and we were marched up to the gym for Battle PT in the morning, then drill, but we all got bagged for one thing or another – boots not clean enough, rooms not tidy enough, etc. After lunch we were marched up to Vimy Barracks for the first of two bayonet courses.

There were human-shaped dummies hanging up in a field, and the Sergeant was shouting at us, "What's the bayonet for?" We all screamed back, "Kill! Kill! Kill!" This went on for a good 20 minutes, then we were shown how to stab the dummy. We had to shout, "On guard!", then stab the dummy with the bayonet attached to the rifle, shouting, "Kill! Kill! Kill!" And we had to do that every time we stabbed it.

It was a three-hour lesson, during which the instructor also told us about the bayonet and how there was a blood channel on it. When you stab the enemy, it inserts a pocket of air into the victim's blood stream, which would kill them if the stab wound didn't. The bayonet is also ridged on the bottom of the blade, which will break the victim's ribs. However, we were shown to twist the bayonet into the enemy before pulling it out, as this would then stop the wound from healing, and the victim's chances of surviving a bayonet attack were next to nothing.

We were run ragged that afternoon, stabbing multiple dummies while dressed as enemy soldiers. We were all filthy and wet, and afterwards we were all fucked, but it was a great afternoon.

The next day, it was back to normal training. The platoon was starting to look like real soldiers.

Chapter 13

NBC Training

Nobody enjoyed nuclear biological chemical (NBC) training, as it was a total lick out every lesson. We would always get in full NBC kit with respirator, then made to run laps of the field and do press-ups. Usually, at least one of us was sick.

One afternoon, we were asked if we would like an afternoon playing football. Everyone said yes, but they failed to mention we had to be in full NBC kit (full Romeo) so that was a hard game of football! I will say one thing for NBC kit, when it's cold outside, it is the best warm kit the British Army issues!

Chapter 14
Drinking With The Lads

We were coming on well in training, and the instructors were true to their word that if we put in the hard work, we would be stood down from Friday to Sunday. I went home a few times, but it was a long way so we regularly got a B&B in Darlington and went out on the piss. One night, I was in the pizza shop when I actually bumped into a girl I had met the year before on holiday in Spain. We had got on really well on holiday and kept in touch for a while before losing contact. That night I was totally shit-faced, took her number, and lost it at some point in the evening. I forgot her surname and never saw her out again, so that was that.

Most of our nights ended up in Route 66 – a nightclub where all the local lads and girls went, along with half of Catterick garrison. Most nights ended with a punch-up involving different regiments, or locals who were pissed off with us trying to nick their girls, which I'm sure was a pain in the arse.

One night we had a bloody fight with a load of trainee Paras who shared our block. It started inside Route 66 and carried on into the street until the local and Military Police turned up. We all ran off laughing, and even shared taxis back to camp. It was just a laugh, no-one died, and we all shook hands and argued who won the fight (of course it was us!).

On the Monday morning, word got around, and our angry Sergeant said to us, "If those SHIT HEADS haven't got black eyes like you, I will beat you all again!" As he walked off, we all stood in silence in three ranks. Minutes later, he came back round with a Parachute Regiment Sergeant, and they were both laughing. They looked at us, then the Para walked off. Our Sergeant said, "Ok, you lot did ok. They all look in a shit state as well. Don't let it happen again, and don't get caught!" He then gave us a wink and told us to go inside.

I was talking to a lad in my platoon who was married, and he told me he would be getting a house from the Army (married quarters) when he passed out and got to his Battalion. That made me think. I really fancied my own pad rather than living with four guys in a room, so I decided to get engaged and planned to get married by the time I got to my Battalion. It seemed like a good idea at the time, but turned out to be the biggest mistake of my life.

Chapter 15
Bayonet – Course Two

On the day leading up to our main bayonet assault course, we got fucking hammered by our Section Commanders. First, we had a room and locker inspection at 0630 hours, then we had two PT sessions. The first, at 0800, was a hard battle PT lesson for an hour, then we had arms drill. But we all got bagged for our kit and told to show at the guard room at 2200. After lunch we had NBC training, followed by PT session two – a tab around the training area in full kit, with 55lbs and weapons.

Because we all failed the room and locker inspection, with most items flying out the window, we had to have another room and locker inspection at 2000 hours, and again we failed. We all then marched to the guard room for our show clean at 2200, feeling very pissed off. We finished the show clean by 2230, but our night was not complete. All through the night we had inspections of the accommodation, and a room and locker check at 0700 in full drill kit. However, our electricity and hot water were turned off that night without us knowing, so we had no way of ironing our clothes, and had to shave in freezing cold water. We were very pissed off.

At 0700, we all stood outside in drill kit, and it was freezing. The Section Commanders came out of the block with fire hoses and soaked the fuck out of us. "Fucking get in there and change into PT kit. You have two minutes," we were told. So, we all ran to our rooms and got changed. We were then speed marched to the gym. There we had a surprise physical fitness training of sit-ups in two minutes, followed by press-ups, then a 1.5-mile run. That was a nightmare at Vimy, because the 400 metres right at the end were up a steep hill.

After PT, we had one hour to get our drill kit sorted and be ready for drill. This meant using another set of kit, because the first one was wet through. We then got hammered on the drill square; we must have marked time for 20 minutes at one point.

We had 30 minutes for lunch, then it was back to the block to change into Combat Fighting Order (CFO) wearing cam cream. We already had weapons and bayonets out for drill. Before marching to the main bayonet assault course, we were asked by the Platoon Sergeant, "Right, lads, are you all nice and pissed off?"

We all shouted, "Yes, Sergeant!"

He then put up his bayonet and shouted, "What's this for?"

"Kill! Kill! Kill!" we all screamed as loud as we could.

He then said to us, "I know you are pissed off, and that was the point of yesterday and today. Now get up there and turn all that pain and hurt into aggression!"

We then marched to Vimy, and every time our left foot hit the tarmac, we shouted, "Kill!"

We had not visited this assault course yet, but it was right at the back end of Vimy, out of the way. It was pissing down with rain, and when we got there, we could hear bagpipes being played. There were loads of smoke and gunfire going off by a GPMG with BAT SIMULATORS, giving the effect of incoming mortars.

This was an individual effort, so we each had to wait our turn. But while waiting, we were made to run and leopard crawl through puddles of mud and shit. I didn't have to wait long before it was my turn.

We had a Sergeant following us, telling us where to go. I had to jump into a freezing cold river and leopard crawl through it with my rifle and bayonet attached. I was looking for dummies dressed as enemy soldiers – some standing up, others lying down in the river. The dummies had been filled with pigs' blood and guts, so every time I stabbed one, all the blood would be all over me and my bayonet. I got really wound up, shouting "Kill!" every time I stabbed the dummies.

I am aware we're talking about stabbing dummies, but the training was preparing us to stab real people to death, to defend our lives and our country. So, you might be wondering if I had any feelings of hesitation or doubt at this point. The answer is no. None whatsoever. In fact, this exercise helped me to release some of the trapped, raging anger that had been building up inside me since I was a child.

Let me explain…

I was born in Welling Garden City in 1985, and my mother Fiona was from Corby, my dad Ian was from Luton. Dad had just left the Army – the Royal Anglian Regiment, who saw action in Northern Ireland and Cyprus in the late 1970s. My mum was a young nanny for a rich family.

Mum and Dad divorced very early in my life, and I moved to Corby with her while Dad went back to Luton.

I didn't see much of my dad, but Mum kept a close bond with his parents, my Nan and Grandad from Luton, so I saw them regularly and was extremely close to them. I also had grandparents on my mum's side (her mum and dad) and a great-grandmother. Throughout my life, my bond with Mum's side was not great, to say the least, apart from my great-grandmother. She never judged me or looked down at me, and would never hear a bad word said about me.

Mum and I lived on an extremely rough council estate named the Exeter, in Corby. Mum was a student, and sometimes had so little money that she would go hungry just so she could feed me. I went to the local infant school on the estate up until it was time to go to primary school.

Until I was around the age of nine years old, it was just me and Mum, and even as a young child I felt like I had to protect her because we lived in a shithole. I don't remember much of infant school, but I recall my primary school (Studfall Juniors in Corby). It was at the other end of town, at least 1.5 miles away, and Mum and I walked it every day because she could not afford the bus fare. Usually, after school my great-gran would pick me up and we would walk to her bungalow on the OAP residents' estate, where I would eat her nuts and wait for Mum.

I would spend most weekends in Luton, where Nan and Grandad would spoil me, taking me out and treating me to holidays. They also took me abroad on trips to Florida, Spain, and France, so in that respect I was lucky. The holidays carried on till I was 14, when I probably became a handful as well as there being other grandchildren on the scene.

By the time I was nine, I was no angel at all. I would be hanging round the streets of the council estate with older lads and girls, experimenting in drinking alcohol. All my friends smoked, but for some reason it never appealed to me. I think it was because Mum smoked, and I hated the smell. We would go to the local shop and nick sweets, start fights, and generally piss off people a lot older than us by garden hopping, knocking doors and running away, or simply by making noise outside someone's house while sitting on their wall. I got more than a few clips around the ear, I can tell you, but it never stopped us.

One day, I was in the back garden shooting milk bottles off the wall with my bow and arrow when my mum came out, told me off, and asked me to meet her friend, who I will refer to as Mr A. I remember he picked me up and said hello.

I didn't really understand what was going on, as I was only nine, but he started spending a lot of time with Mum at our house. He was the brother of Mum's friend, who lived just a few doors away, and I knew he had kids that also lived on the estate as well. I think at the time I really just wanted a father figure in my life, as I didn't have one apart from Grandad, and he lived in Luton.

Mum fell pregnant with my sister before I was 10 years old. When she was over four months into her pregnancy, I was sitting playing in the living room one day when I heard a loud knock on the front door. I opened the door and there stood Mum's friend – the new man's sister – and she was shouting, "Get your fucking mum, I want your fucking mum!"

Mum came to the door, and the bitch attacked her while she was pregnant, in front of me. I tried to defend my mum but was knocked out the way, so I went into the kitchen and picked up a large knife and ran outside, ready to stab the bitch that was hurting my mum. By the time I got outside, Mr A was on the scene. He must have been following his sister, as he had a hold of her, while Mum grabbed me, took the knife off me, led me inside and shut the door. I am 32 years old now, but I still remember that so clearly. And it was the start of fucking hell for seven or eight years. It had been going on before this incident, but Mum had been able to hide the shit from me. After that, though, I was wise to it, and no way was I going to let some fucker hurt my mum again.

I was in Luton when she went into labour with my sister. The baby was very premature, and Mum was also very poorly; at one point, it looked like they both might die, so I spent lots of time by Mum's bed in hospital and looking in at my sister, who was in an incubator. Luckily, they both survived, though the baby had to remain in hospital for some time.

It was when my sister got home that I remember things really started to change. Mr A would hardly be there, and when he was, he was always shouting at Mum. I would go downstairs and tell him to leave her alone, and usually he would just storm out and slam the door.

One day, Mum and I were walking to the local shop, as she needed some bits. Mr A was at home, so he stayed with his baby daughter. Mum wanted to go to a shop that was a bit farther away, which was a bit of a walk, but I suppose it was because Mr A was being a fucker again. On our way back home, we could see an ambulance outside our house, so we ran back just as the ambulance drove away.

My sister had suffered a major brain bleed and was rushed to Kettering General Hospital. She was less than six months old and put on life support. Luckily, she pulled through, but she suffered brain damage as a direct result. Mr A was arrested for Grievous Bodily Harm (GBH) but later released, and he, of course, denied any responsibility. But back then Mum was young and in love, so she believed him and took him back.

When we moved with him from Corby to live in rented accommodation on the Ise Lodge in Kettering, I started to see what he was really like. I had to move schools, so I was enrolled at Millbrook Primary School. I was really starting to struggle at school around this age, particularly with spelling and numbers, but I just thought I was as thick as shit, so I started misbehaving in class to hide the fact that I was struggling.

Because I had lived life up until this point in Corby, I had a plastic Scottish accent. And even though Kettering is only ten miles from Corby, the accent is totally different. This made it fairly difficult to settle in with different friends, not to mention the rivalry back then between the two towns. Life was also very different in Kettering, and pastimes such as nicking from the local shop, starting fights, or smashing windows at the age of ten or 11, were unheard of. So I had to find other hobbies, like football and girls.

Mr A worked away a lot of the time which suited me, because I hated the man. All he seemed to do when he was at home was shout at Mum and treat her like a piece of shit. It was while we were living there that she fell pregnant again, with my brother. I couldn't wait to have a baby brother as well as a sister.

My own dad from Luton was back on the scene around this time. He had been in prison for a while, for knocking out two police officers, but I didn't know that at the time. My dad was well connected to the Luton gang world and was not to be messed with; in fact, some of his best friends were doing time for armed bank jobs and killing a police officer. It made me feel a bit safer knowing he wasn't that far away, and I really let Mr A know about it.

When my brother was born, nothing changed. In fact, Mr A got worse. He was constantly shouting at Mum and my brother and sister, throwing all their toys around the house, but he would always leave me alone.

One afternoon when I was 12, he was kicking off, smashing up the house, and Mum was in tears. So, I went outside, picked up a brick, and put it through his car windscreen, which stopped the fight. I said to him, "Come on then, I'll fight you." But he got in his car and fucked off at speed, then I got a bollocking off my mum for smashing the shitbag's windscreen.

My brother suffered a broken leg as an infant, when Mr A was looking after him; apparently, he fell down the stairs. Bullshit is what I say to that, but my brother was too young to know what happened. The man was a fucking bully.

When I was 13, we moved from the rented accommodation. Mum and the bully managed to get a mortgage, as she had a government-funded job and he also worked full time. So we moved into a nice house (Mum is still there to this day) on the Ise Lodge, which meant I didn't need to move schools. I was just leaving my primary school going to secondary school – Latimer School, which was about a mile from the new house.

It was at the new house that things got out of hand. The bully was out of control at home, and I would often sit upstairs looking after my brother and sister while he would be downstairs, shouting and smashing the house up, then the Police would be called. That was pretty much life at home for me.

School wasn't much better. Me and my mates would meet up at the spinney and walk through the field to Latimer School, but I was still struggling with my work. So, I acted up in class to hide the fact that I couldn't read, spell, or work with numbers.

Eventually, Mum got a restraining order against the bully, preventing him from coming near us. But even that didn't stop him. I would regularly see his car parked round the corner from our house, so I would get a baseball bat from my room and chase the car off.

I also had a powerful air rifle which my dad had bought me. At one point I shot my friend in the head from 10 metres. It was a total mistake, because I didn't think there was a pellet loaded. Luckily, it didn't hit him directly, just grazing his head and missing his eye.

One day I got back from school and could see my bedroom window was open, but I knew Mum wasn't at home. I ran to the house where I found the fucker's car outside and him sitting in the living room in silence, his electric guitar in his hand. I asked him, "What the fuck are you doing here, you fucking twat? Get out!"

He just sat in silence and ignored me. I tried to call Mum, but the downstairs phone wires had been disconnected. Thinking back, I was probably scared shitless, because I thought I could fight then, but no way could a child fight a grown man.

I left him in the living room and sat on the stairs to wait for Mum. Luckily, she usually got home shortly after me, but she had no idea he was there until she saw his car. As she came rushing in with the two toddlers, I told her he was in the living room, so she took my brother and sister upstairs and asked me to play with them.

I didn't want to leave my mum, but I went in my room with them to wait. After a few minutes I heard Mum and him in the bedroom arguing. I had a lock outside my bedroom door up high, and I would lock it when I was out, so that my siblings couldn't go into my room. However, the bully must have locked it once we were inside, because after a few minutes I heard them in the bedroom arguing then they went downstairs. All I could hear was Mum getting hurt, glass being broken, and things being smashed. But when I went to open my door, it was locked.

I kicked the shit out of my door until I managed to open it, and ran down the stairs, but I couldn't get into the living room because the TV had been thrown against the door. After kicking that door, I managed to get through, and I jumped in front of Mum, throwing punches at him. He went upstairs and jumped out of one of the windows, hitting the ground, but then came back through the front door before we could close it in time. This time he came back up the stairs, going fucking mad.

There was a big struggle at the top of the stairs, and it looked like he jumped head-first down the stairs. I was hoping the fucker was dead! Mum went to see if he was ok and told me to try the bedroom phone to call for help. It was working, but I thought *Fuck him!* and called my gran and grandad (Mum's parents) as they lived just five minutes away.

When they turned up maybe 30 minutes later, I was upstairs looking after my crying brother and sister. But then I heard it all start again, so I took my baseball bat, went down the stairs, and saw Mr A with his hands around Grandad's neck, trying to steal all the house keys! I hit him round the back of the head, and he dropped the keys and ran out of the house, while I followed him out, swinging my bat at his car as he left.

I'm not sure who called them, but the Police turned up a few minutes later with their blues and twos on. Unbelievably, when they got him, he tried making a complaint against me for assault and criminal damage.

I had to leave for Luton and stay at my Nan and Grandad's house for three weeks after this. It was the only place I felt safe. While I was there, my dad called me and asked, "Ben, where is that fucker living right now? Enough is enough."

I won't go into details, but let's just say that since the fright my dad and his friends gave him, I have never seen him again. However, I am in my thirties and still have nightmares and issues with people being in the house today.

Even though he had gone, I wasn't convinced that he would not come back. So, literally every day when I got home from school, I would get out my air rifle and a knife I kept hidden under the stairs, then check the house from top to bottom to make sure no-one was there.

Life settled into more of a routine when he left, as there were no fights in the house other than me being given regular bollockings from Mum for getting into trouble. I was still struggling at school, and when I was put into the Special Needs Department (SND), I was so embarrassed. There would be times when I was sitting in class and a teacher would come and call my name out, so I would have to get up and go to SND. I hated it, and used to avoid it like the plague. On top of that, I was still experiencing anxiety when I was on my way home, wondering if there would be a visitor waiting.

Even though Mr A had left my life, the anger and resentment never did. So, years later, on that day when I was crawling through all the pigs' blood and stabbing the fuck out of the dummies, in my mind it was the bully's head on the dummies, and I got through the bayonet assault course with pure adrenalin. At one point I took the bayonet off the rifle and stabbed the fuck out of one of the dummies, shouting, "Die, you fucker, die!" Only I knew who I was thinking of. I was covered in blood and shit by the end, and shaking from the adrenalin, but I loved it. In fact, it was one of the best expe-riences I have ever had, even to this day.

Once it was over, we walked – not marched – back to Helles barracks, where we cleaned our rifles and bayonets before handing them in. It was a Friday, and we had the weekend off. I went home for a few days to see family and friends, but was so wound up from the bayonet course that I got really drunk on the way home and ended up in a fight in Kettering town – just for a change.

Chapter 16
Battlefield Tour – Week Sixteen

We had a real treat when we were taken to Belgium for a battlefield tour and to the Menin Gate ceremony that happens every evening. We drove there by bus, then got the ferry, for the two-night trip. During that time, we visited the trenches from WW1, and went to some of the battlefields where brave young men and boys gave their lives. Some had been as young as 14 and had lied about their age so that they could join up to fight. Some gravestones say, 'Unknown Soldier', and it was a very sad and eye-opening experience to see how many people died, and at such a young age!

At the Menin Gate, there are thousands of soldiers named around the bridge, and hundreds of people turn up every night to show respect for the sacrifice made by these brave young men. I had the privilege of wearing my number two dress as I marched with four others and laid a wreath to honour those who lost their lives.

That night some of us snuck out of the hotel, went clubbing in the local town, and got totally plastered. One of our Section Commanders was also out, and at one point we ended up in the same pub as him. He said, "Lads, I never saw you tonight. Don't get caught out."

We ended up having a punch-up with some local lads, because we were trying to chat up their girls whilst drunk, and in a totally different language! No wonder they hated us! But it wasn't my first rodeo. We got lost on the way back to the hotel and just made it back about one hour before we all had to be up.

Word had got out that we had been on the razz, and the Platoon Sergeant had us by our necks, screaming at us. We just took the bollocking and never mentioned that we had seen another Sergeant and that he knew we had been out. Big boys' rules do count for something.

Chapter 17
Military Fitness Tests

From week one of training, we were gradually building up our stamina to sit the mandatory fitness test and pass out as Infantry soldiers. Because we were Guards, the standard was higher than that of a regular Infantry unit.

By the time we were in the last quarter towards the end of training, we had really improved our fitness. The PTI was concentrating on our Combat Fitness Test (CFT), which is a loaded march/run (TAB) with 55 pounds in your Burgan and webbing, then we had the extra weight of our helmets (which had to be worn), water, and our personal weapons. The Tab was eight miles long and had to be completed in less than two hours. The official time for the Infantry CFT is two hours, but we were told we had to raise the standard and complete it in 1 hour 30 minutes (it was all psychological). I found the best thing to do was carry a chocolate bar and have a bite at each water stop; it's amazing how much energy you could get from it.

At the start of training, Tabs were shorter and less weight was carried, but we were nearing the end of the course so we were pushing eight miles a Tab and further.

One morning at 07.30, we went for a Tab with 55 pounds plus weapons, water, and our helmets. We got fucking hammered around the back door training area, and pretty much ran the whole thing. There is a hill called 'Land of Nod', which is basically a small mountain that is as steep as you like going up. The track was also just rocks and dirt, so keeping our footing was a nightmare and lots of guys got injured there. We went up and down the Land of Nod twice on that Tab, then carried on round the area, and on the way back had the total joy of going back up the Land of Nod for the third time that session. Everyone who finished the Tab (some guys fell behind and got put in the Jack wagon) was totally fucked. I was physically sick going up the Land of Nod for the third time!

The PTI separated us from the guys who never completed it, and told us, "Well done, troops, we have just completed 12 miles there. So, next week on your CFT, you should have no fucking trouble! You lazy twats who got in the Jack wagon want to have a long hard look in the mirror. If you don't pass next week, you don't pass out!"

As we then walked in step the mile back to Helles barracks, it meant that in total we had completed a 14-miler.

Chapter 18

First Aid and
Other Training

I have forgotten to mention First Aid, which is a big part of being an Infantry soldier. We learnt First Aid all through our time in training, doing a couple of lessons a day, and had regular testing on being the first person on scene – known as Battle First Aid. I enjoyed this, and it was something that would come in very handy in the future.

We also did a lot of map reading and orienteering, though I wasn't the strongest map reader, to be honest. I was okay when out on the ground, as I could relate the map to the surroundings, but when it came to doing map and compass lessons in a classroom with the Platoon Commander (officer), I wouldn't have a clue what he was on about, and found it hard to stay awake because he was so fucking boring! Now, looking back, it was my dyslexia which was the problem in a classroom with trying to orientate the map and understand things like contours, while I found it so much easier on the ground.

I think it's compulsory in the Guards for officers to teach map reading in a warm classroom and to make it as long and as boring as possible, because it was always the same, even in Battalion. I learnt so much more when out on the ground with physical landmarks.

The other really boring lesson we had to do in a classroom was learning about the radios we used, like the personal role radio (PRR) which lets you talk to members of your section and Section Commander. We also learned about the types of radios used by the Army at that time, how to connect them up, and how to use the correct frequency to send situation reports to each other (SIT REPS). Again, boring as fuck! The instructor didn't help, with his monotone voice and double chin; it was clear why he was in charge of radios! In my view, it was another lesson that should be explained out on the ground, but we don't all have the same way of learning in life. I suppose teaching would be much easier if that was the case.

I much preferred to be outside with hands-on learning, and I'm the same to this day. I'm sure it is because of my dyslexia, because I learn fuck all by sitting listening to someone trying to teach, unless it's in the moment. But as I say, not everyone is the same, and the instructors were only following the pamphlet of training.

Chapter 19
NBC Test

This was shit. It was a test to see how long it took us to go from having just regular kit on to NBC, and we were given two minutes. Once we had done it, we got sent to the football pitch to run from goal post to goal post, doing a press-up every time we reached the halfway line. After about 20 minutes of this shit, we could stop and take off the respirators to get our breath back, and then it was into the gas chamber. This is a small room with sealed windows, a concrete floor, and a big door sealing you in, with no gaps.

We went in without respirators on, but had them in our pouches. And we knew what was coming next! The door shut and there was a Section Commander standing there. He then let off CS gas pellets, shouting "Gas! Gas! Gas!" We then pulled out our respirators and put them on, shouting "Gas! Gas! Gas!" when they were on. If you were not quick enough, you would start to choke badly, and your eyes would water. We had to then make sure each other's NBC kit was fitted properly, otherwise the CS gas would burn the skin – not enough to really hurt you, but you would certainly feel it.

Once this was complete, we had to stay in the gas chamber for about ten minutes while the Section Commander kept setting off more CS pellets.

At the end, we each took off our respirator in front of the Sergeant, ate a piece of ration pack biscuit, then shouted our name, rank, and Army number. We were then ushered out of the gas chamber, where there was another instructor waiting with a bucket of water to dunk our heads in. This helped our eyes to stop stinging. Everyone was coughing, and snot was all over our faces. It was funny watching others come out of the gas chamber; I suppose it was funny all round, really.

Chapter 20

Steeple Chase

This is a combat assault course that stretches out for two miles, and it's a best individual effort with us all setting off at different times. We were shown around the course in advance, but on the day of the steeple chase, it was snowing.

When it was my turn to set off, I gave it 110%. We had to leopard crawl through shit and puddles, and at one point you have to hold your breath while you go through a dark tunnel full of water, where an instructor is waiting for you at the other end in case you don't come out. The rest of the course has a wall to go over, nets to climb, and a river to go through, covered in ice and snow. There were also many obstacles in the way, such as razor wire you needed to crawl under, and holes you needed to jump in. And it is not just ground-based; at some points, you are also up in the trees.

I completed the course in 18 minutes, by which time I was piss wet through and covered from head to toe in shit. Once we came in, we were shown to the gym changing rooms and told to strip and put dry clothes on.

I was sick at the finish line and couldn't stop shaking for at least ten minutes. To be honest, we were all in bits after the steeple chase, but it was fun.

Chapter 21
Observation Posts

We had a few lessons on how to build an Observation Post (OP). An OP is basically a very well camouflaged watch post where we can get close to the enemy without them knowing we are there. Life in Ops can be very uncomfortable at times (as I found out later on hostile operations), and there can be two or four men in the OP. You are on a hard routine the whole time, which means you have to eat cold meals, you cannot talk, and you piss and shit in bags. There is no white light or flames used to cook or keep warm, as this can and will compromise your position.

The reasoning behind OPs is to gather enemy information such as manpower, weapons, used vehicles, and their morale. Some OPs can be so close to the enemy that you can hear them talking, see their faces, and even smell their food.

This is why hard routine is very important, not only to gather enemy's information but to stay alive.

Chapter 22
Fighting In Built-Up Areas (FIBUCA)

This was a one-week training in how to operate and fight in built-up areas such as streets and towns. It was fun, but we could not believe how fucking hard it was. It is a lot more complicated than doing simple section and platoon attacks in the field. We learned how to tactically enter buildings, as well as to give fire support if that's the role we took. Usually, one section would give cover fire, while another section assaulted buildings and positions. We would try not to go through obvious entry points like windows, because they would likely be rigged with explosives, so we would use mouse charges and blow a hole in a wall. (As this was training, we would just demonstrate it, then use a window.)

It would then be on to room clearances, and the usual standard operating procedure is to pop a high explosive grenade into the room, or a flash bang. After the explosion, you and a team member would enter the room, tactically firing and killing any enemy there, then another team would go to the next room, and so on. When the building was secure, the covering sections would move forward and take over the assault, while getting cover from the previous assaulting sections. Like I say, it was hard graft, but we all enjoyed it. And it proved to be valuable training for what lay ahead in Iraq and Afghanistan.

It was surprising how many real-life casualties we got just during training, due to guys falling off ladders, getting caught up in razor wire, and all sorts of hazards. So, you can imagine how dangerous this is when it's for real.

Chapter 23

Riot Training
Against the Police

This was a real treat. It was over a weekend, but we didn't care, because we could still go out on the drink at night. It consisted of 21 of the Platoon acting as angry rioters for Police training for two days, and it's fair to say we took it seriously. There were a number of times we would break through their lines and single out the weak members, dragging them to the floor and giving them a few light slaps. The exercise had to be stopped and restarted quite a lot throughout the two days.

Initially, we could throw stones, but as the adrenalin increased, so did the missiles we threw at them. In the end, we were given wooden blocks the size of bricks, and that's all we were allowed to throw. At the end of each day – fair play to them – they supplied us all with a takeaway, and when the second day was over, we got a big thank you from the Police Inspector of the unit. We certainly gave them as much of a good kicking as we were allowed to. It was fun.

Chapter 24

Combat Fitness Test (CFT)

Although we had smashed a 12-miler the week before, I was still nervous on the day of the official CFT. I think it's just in the back of your mind that you could get injured or have an off day. If you failed the CFT, you were allowed one more attempt two days later, and if you failed that you would be put into a platoon behind you and had to redo parts of training. If you had an injury, however, you would go to Williams Company – a rehabilitation platoon – and if you recovered there, you would be put in a platoon going through training and still have to redo a lot of the training.

At 0800, we had our kit weighed by our Section Commanders. Each man had 55 pounds in his Burgan and webbing, not including his personal water, helmet, and personal weapon system (SA80). Once we were all checked, we tabbed the one mile to Vimy Barracks, where the CFT started outside the gym. The PTI was waiting for us, and we had our kit weighed for the second time in case some off the lads had tried to blag it and get rid of some of the weight on the way up to the gym. Once we were all checked, we had our warm-up on the football field for ten minutes.

It was then time to set off in three ranks. We started fairly quickly, breaking into double march (running) soon after starting, then we went up the dreaded Land of Nod and carried on with our CFT route. We never knew how far we had gone because the routes were always different. The only thing that never changed was the Jack wagon behind us and the Section Commanders gobbing off. We always had to have two hands on our weapon in training; if we were caught with a hand off the weapon, or talking, we would be made to run around the squad as many times as the PTI felt fit. This doesn't sound too harsh, but believe me it is, so it was wise not to be caught out.

We had two water stops on the CFT, and I had a bite of my chocolate bar at each stop. On the way back in, we went up the Land of Nod again, and we came in just over one-and-a-half hours, giving us just under 30 minutes to spare. There were a few lads who had to bin it off and get in the Jack wagon, and they had to redo their CFT, but the second one was done in two hours – the time allowed by the Army. Unfortunately, there were two lads who failed and had to be put back in platoons behind us.

For those of us who passed, it would not be the final TAB (CFT) we had to do; they just got harder. But at least we had passed the main CFT military test.

After the CFT had been completed, we still had Final EX/ battle camp and two weeks of royal duties, and of course shitloads more PT, along with a room and locker inspection at least twice a day. As per every day in training, we would have a personal inspection every morning of whatever uniform we had to wear that day. And just like day one, week one – if you failed, it was 2200 hours at the guard room. If you got bagged for three things, you would be given an extra guard duty – usually over a weekend, which messed up going out with the lads, or night duty before a hard PT session.

Chapter 25
Final Exercise

March 2004

Our last blank firing exercise of training was held in the Scottish Highlands, and we would be in the field for the whole two weeks. It was a good four-hour drive to the area, and from the moment we arrived there the weather was a mix of sleet and snow, and fucking freezing.

Within our sections, we had all support small arms weapons such as LMG/GPMG/LSW drill LAW, and regular rifle men had their SA80s. We all shared kit accordingly, with things like ammo for the support weapons, water, and sandbags. We each carried 48 hours of rations, personal water, personal ammo training grenades, and spare kit, including a basher to sleep under and an issued bouncing bomb (sleeping bag), with a bivvy bag to keep the sleeping bag dry.

Our orders were that we had to do a 48-hour advance to contact as a platoon effort, moving in sections – two up, one back in reserve. The terrain was the worst I had experienced in my life; it was boggy, with your feet sinking with every step, sometimes as much as waist-deep. It was also full of little bumps which you could lose your footing on (babies' heads). We called this a total lick-out – basically, we were fucked physically and mentally.

As a platoon we advanced across the moors, clearing pockets of enemy along the way. This is where all our training came into play, and even though it was only a blank exercise, we had to take it very seriously and be 100% tactical at all times. We would be resupplied with ammo and rations, and designated rendezvous and check points. We would never stay in the same harbour area to rest, as the mission exercise was to advance north, clearing out pockets of enemy forces. We also sent out RECCE screens to log what the enemy's strengths were, as well as their morale.

After the first week-and-a-half of lack of sleep and miles of tabbing through the moors clearing enemy, we made a harbour area where we were told we would stay for around 48 hours, in order to resupply and send out RECCE screens at night to log enemy activity. This meant we could all do our two-hour stag duties around the clock, while the rest of the troops sorted their personal admin, had a good meal, and got some rest.

Resupply turned up with rations, but we were told, "Sorry, lads, the convoy was ambushed on route to RV point, so we have no water for at least 24 hours!"

Clearly this was just part of the game, so we had to make do with using snow on the ground and melting it to drink. We also got water from the local river, used our purifying tablets, then boiled the water to kill any shit that was more than likely still in it.

This was just a test to see how we got on, because after roughly ten hours of melting snow, we had our water resupply, along with egg banjos per man. It was like deepest fantasy, a dream come true (amazing)!

Our final exercise was carried on at high intensity, but this was to be expected. It consisted of advance to contacts, fighting patrols, ambushes, reconnaissance patrols, and not much sleep or down time.

The final 48 hours of the exercise was good. We sent out a RECCE party to observe the remaining enemy forces who were defending an old Navy port, and this was going to be our final platoon attack.

We got our orders in our harbour area and were told we would move off on foot at 0001 and advance to the Navy port. No pockets of enemy had been spotted by the RECCE screen up till the port. The Tab in was honking; it was pissing down with rain. At one point I sank into a bog up to my neck and had to be pulled out. People have gone hiking around there never to be seen again, or so I have heard, and I can believe it after that horrible experience. Every member of the platoon was piss wet through and fucked.

The Tab was six kilometres but felt like about 50 due to the rain. We all formed in, using one section as fire support and the other two as the assaulting force. My section was one of the chosen assaulting sections.

Then we waited in the bun line, in the pissing rain, waiting for the sun to rise for our dawn attack (H Hour).

The final attack was a success, from the feedback we got in the debrief, but as always there is room for improvement. We were just glad to have got the final exercise out of the way, though. It was a really tough exercise, but by now we had learned how to sustain ourselves in the field, and most of all it was real soldiering.

Now there were only two phases of training battle camp left – the main Infantry battle tests (if you failed this, you could not pass out with your platoon), and the two-week royal duty phase.

Chapter 26

Battle Camp

Battle camp is based in Warcop in Cumbria, and this course was all live firing ranges with all weapon systems we had been trained on – SA80, GPMG (machine gun), LMG (machine gun), and LAW (anti-tank weapon). It also included the live HE grenade, and it was a one-week course. We had to run everywhere we went, instead of marching, and were in full combat fighting order (CFO) when on the ranges.

The first couple of days were spent on the ranges, shooting at moving targets from different firing positions, and through and over obstacles. We then started to put pairs fire, and moving to practise advancing down a range, shooting pop-up targets, working as a team with one giving cover while the other moved. It then developed to four-man teams' fire and moving, with two giving cover and two advancing.

You have to remember that if a mistake was made, there was a high possibility of a soldier being shot, even with all the safety measures put in place. And it would not have been the first, or last, time someone would be injured – in some cases, fatally!

We worked our way up to section live attacks at this point, giving covering fire while a designated Grenadier posted a live HE grenade into an enemy position. (Clearly, because we were using live ammo, the enemy were metal targets that fell when hit.) All this was preparing us for our final live platoon assault at the end of the week.

We had another eight-mile Tab, although it was not a combat fitness test while at battle camp. It was to get us used to all the support weapons and ammo and water we would need to carry into battle. Carrying the extra kit made a big difference, but we were now combat fit, so even though it hurt, we all passed. We were all so close to passing out that we really didn't want to fuck it up now after six hard months of training.

Chapter 27

Two-Miler APWT (Shooting Test)

On the second to last day, we had the two-miler, followed by APWT, which was hard. It is a TAB/RUN to the 400-metre range. You start at 100 metres, and your breathing is all over the place from the two-miler, then you do various shoots in different positions – prone, standing, kneeling, sitting targets fall when hit.

We then heard "GAS! GAS! GAS!", so had to run back to the 200-metre point, get in the trench provided, and carry on the respirator shoot. Everyone was blowing out their arse at this point! Next it was the respirator off and we had to double back to the 300-metre point to fire in the prone position, then back to the 400-metre point for the final shoot of the range.

We also had shooting tests on the GMPG and LMG – the support weapons.

Chapter 28
Final Battle Camp Exercise

This was it, the big one. If we got through this, we were qualified Infantry soldiers. We then just needed to pass the ceremonial side of being in the Guards.

It was a full platoon attack with live rounds. We were at the line of departure just before dawn, and we heard the live mortars being fired in. This was a good experience hearing mortars flying over our heads (of course, they were being fired in a safe direction, but it gave a good effect). Then came the fire support from a GPMG being fired well over our heads and off to a safe direction, but you could hear the thud and crack. This was the sign that it was H hour, and the platoon attack started on the objective.

The attack and reorg lasted about three hours and it was hard graft, but we got good training out of the whole exercise. We all mucked in and cleaned the weapons on the bus on way back to Catterick, as it was a Friday. I needed to go home, and others needed a beer.

Chapter 29
Final Two Weeks –
Ceremonial Training

We had passed all military annual training tests to be an Infantry soldier, but now we had two weeks of bullshit, learning royal duties and getting our pass-out parade perfect.

We were up at 0500 every day, with a drill kit inspection, PT at 0800, then arms drill for the rest of the day, learning what we needed to know for ceremonial duties outside the royal palace. Some lads from different Guards were going to be going to their Battalion to do royal duties. However, I was lucky, because my Battalion had an Iraq deployment coming up in 2005, so they needed the manpower. I was so happy to find out I was going to Iraq, I felt like a little kid waiting for Santa.

But I still had to do the royal training anyway. I'm not going to lie, drill was not my strong point at all. I was much more a green soldier, but I cracked on and got there in the end – after about a week's worth of 2200 hour show parades. (That didn't include the previous six months' worth of show clean parades!)

It was the Friday, and we were due to pass out on the Thursday of the following week. We'd had a nightmare of a day on the drill square and were all tired and pissed off, so we needed to be allowed to fall out for the weekend. Me and a lad from the Grenadier Guards had never seen eye to eye, and that day it came to blows outside the Armoury. He gave me an elbow across the jaw, but it didn't really take much effect. I then hit him a good five times before we were split up by the other lads. It was all over very quickly, and I thought that was the end of it. But some fucker grassed us up.

I was in my room when my Section Commander shouted to me, "Close! Get in the drying room!" When I walked in, I saw he had the other lad in there as well.

He told us, "Right, you shits, you want to fight? Because I'm going to the NAAFI and locking this door behind me. Big boys' rules. Get on with it. No-one to stop you both now!"

As he left and locked the door, we both looked at each other, and I said, "Okay, you wanna fight? Get this shit sorted as men?"

He put out his hand and said, "No, Ben, it's done. My jaw hurts, and I want to go home tonight." I shook his hand and that was that.

When our Sergeant came back in, he called us both fannies and told us if it happened again, we would be fighting him! To this day, I think this Sergeant was a cold, nasty bastard, but I truly believe he is a fantastic soldier who deals with things like that in the right way. I am glad I had him as a Section Commander, and today as a friend. (I worked with him again years later in Afghanistan in 2007, after passing out of training, and again as a close protection officer in 2018.)

Finally, we were all ready to pass out on Thursday, April 23, 2004 – St George's Day!

Chapter 30
Pass-Out Parade

23rd April, 2004, St. George's Day

We had a full dress rehearsal the day before, and the night before pass-out, all the troops were up till sparrow-a-fart, making sure all our kit was perfect.

Everything in our kit was handed in that day except No.2 dress, which is our smart green uniform (I actually wore this for my first wedding as well!), and a set Combat 95 uniform. The rest was to be shipped to our respective Battalions. But things like webbing and helmets, CBA, Burgans, sleeping bags, and ponchos, were all handed back into the stores, as we would be given new kit at our units.

Morning of pass-out

After breakfast at 0630, we had another rehearsal but only in combats, and got a good thrashing (I guess it was their last chance!). Family started to arrive early, but we could not meet them until we had passed off the drill square as qualified Guardsmen.

We had all our civvy kit packed and ready to go on our beds, all sheets and pillows had been handed in, and accommodation inspected and handed over. So, this meant that as soon as we finished pass out, we could meet family in the

NAAFI, have a drink, and go home on two weeks of well deserved leave before joining our respective battalions.

We all formed up outside the block in No2 dress, drill boots that you could see your face in, buff belts that were gleaming, and immaculate forage caps. Every part of our kit was in perfect order. The night before we had all mucked in together, helping those who were weaker at some bits of kit but would be better at others.

At 1030 we had a routine inspection by our Platoon Sergeant. He praised us on our hard work throughout, and told us now was our chance to shine. I remember him saying, "This is your day, lads."

The band started, and that was our key to step onto the drill square. My heart – and I'm sure the others felt the same – was beating about 1000 beats a minute. We had rehearsed so many times, but this was finally the real thing with thousands of people watching us.

Once we got on the square, however, everything fell into place, the nerves disappeared, and we just went with it.

The MP William Hague was there to inspect us (not that he had any clue what to look for), and he was shown round by the ITC, Commanding Officer. Even on pass-out, if you were in a shit state, you would be in trouble and would be reported to your new unit. And that's not the way to start your unit as a crow (a new soldier).

The pass-out lasted about an hour. We did a combination of arms drill movements, quick march and slow march, going back into quick march – based on a royal parade. At the end of the parade, we all marched past the families, friends, and officers, as well as the MP. We gave an eyes right and a salute on the march with weapons. Then the band sounded, it was all over, and the crowd cheered for us all.

We carried on marching up to the Armoury till we were out of sight of the public, handed in our weapons and bayonets, then marched to the NAAFI to meet our families.

When I walked into the bar, I was met by Mum, my brother and sister, Dad, his brother Steve, Nan (from Dad's side), and Gran and Grandad, as well Great-Gran. We enjoyed a lovely meal and a few well-deserved beers. I got hammered, to be fair, and went home in No.2 dress.

I have not previously mentioned this much, but I was due to be married the week after, while on leave. I knew I didn't love her, because I was not a good boy at this point. I was too young, but I went along with it so that I could get an Army house. I just wanted to prove everyone wrong and to settle down and have the kind of life I had not had as a child or young man. In truth, I was too young, with the wrong person, and so immature for something like marriage. And it would prove to be a massive mistake.

Chapter 31
Leave

My two weeks off went very fast, and at just four weeks over 19 years old, I was about to be married and had a house to move into. And even though I knew deep down it was a huge mistake, I carried on.

The wedding was a joke, to say the least. It was a small registry office job with a party afterwards. A lot of my friends turned up, and we were all hammered. In fact, half-way through the evening, I left my new wife and went out on the town with mates, met a few girls I hadn't seen for a while, and got into a fight with some local lads I didn't like. In my defence, I took my new wife back a cold doner kebab, so fair's fair!

Alarm bells were ringing from the start, but at least I had my house in Aldershot! As I say, it was all very silly and immature.

Chapter 32

Life as a Crow in Aldershot

I moved to Lille Barracks in Aldershot, as a newly-married 19-year-old, alongside only one other lad who had passed out from our regiment. The first day I turned up in a suit, as instructed, and the other guy and I were shown to the training wing, where we met a Sergeant. He told us that before we could be assigned to a company within the Battalion, we had to do a week's worth of refresher training, which basically consisted of all the PT we had passed in training like BFT, CFT, 2-miler, skill-at-arms tests, and bullshit classroom lessons and briefs.

By the end of the week and draft training on the Friday, on the Commanding Officer's orders we were officially welcomed to the Battalion, and told the do's and don'ts.

We were told that the Battalion was split into five companies. Companies 1, 2, and 3 were the Rifle companies (front-line foot soldiers), you then had the Support company (this is where usually the more experienced soldiers are), which consisted of all specialised infantry weapons – 81mm Mortar, Recce, Sniper, Anti-tank, Machine gunners (Mounted GPMG). And finally, there was the Headquarter company, where you get the storemen, drivers, elements of attached REME (Royal Electrical and Mechanical Engineers), Regimental Police, and all high-ranking officers such as the Commanding Officer, his second-in-command the Adjutant, as well as the Badge (Regimental Sergeant Major, RSM).

All companies (depending on military exercises and deployments) took their turn doing barrack guard to protect the camp. If nothing was on, number 1 company would be on guard for seven days, then the following week it changed to another company. But to be honest, it was usually the Rifle companies that got spammed with Barrack Guard and Quick Reaction Force. QRF was a good number, as it lasted 48 hours and there would be two members of the company attached to two other soldiers, located away from our own camp. It was basically assisting the Military Police doing checkpoints and driving around the training area at night, making sure there were no unauthorised personnel on the training area. We were always armed with personal weapon SA80 and ammunition.

We often caught kids on motorbikes and people pissing around on the training area, but as soon as they saw us, they would disappear. However, the amount of people we caught in the middle of the night enjoying a secret rendezvous was too many to count; it was definitely an RV for secret rendezvous around the training area!

During the welcome brief we were also informed that we would be deploying to Iraq in 2005 as a Battalion Battle Group, dates TBC.

I was assigned to Number 2 Company, and my mate was in Number 1 Company. I met my new CSM late on a Friday as he was just leaving the office. I stood to attention and said, "Sir, I am GDSM Close. I have just been put in your Company, sir."

His reply was, "Ya, ya, you're my new guardsman (GDSM), but it's Friday and I am meeting the lads in the mess. So, as you are a PAD (married soldier), get ya arse home, and see you outside my office at 0800 Monday, dressed in good order Combat 95, and we will have a chat. Okay, lad."

"Yes, sir."

"Ok, fuck off, and don't drink too much."

So that was that till Monday. I had already received all my kit from the training camp, so I spent most of the weekend going through it. My house was not too far from camp, so getting kit home was quite easy – just as well, because I hadn't met anyone else yet, so I couldn't, and didn't want to, ask for help.

That weekend, me and the lad I passed out with met up for a drink in town, and we met some of the other lads from the Battalion. At that point, I felt like a small fish in a big pond.

Chapter 33
Life in Number 2 Company

It was the Monday morning, and I was at my company office early to meet the CSM. I waited outside his office for around ten minutes before he turned up, then went in and introduced myself, as did he. He set down the law straight away and assigned me to number 5 platoon.

When I met my Platoon Sergeant and the rest of the platoon, it was quite scary because I knew no fucker at all. Most of the guys had recently finished a tour in Northern Ireland, so I really was the crow bag. It soon became evident that being a married soldier and living in an army house was not the thing to do, as it made it a lot harder to bond with the lads in your company and platoon.

During the first few days of getting to know the lads, one guy – let's call him C – asked me where I lived. When I told him, it turned out he was only a few doors down, so that was my first friend and a lift to work and back every day. The married personnel had a pads room where we could keep our military kit so that we didn't have to bring things into work every day, but it was more like a changing room.

On the Thursday of the first week, I was invited to go out drinking with some members of my platoon in Aldershot, so we went to a few bars then on to the local club, Cheeks. The club was full of young girls and squaddies, and I knew instantly that my marriage was to be short-lived. I must have met at least five girls within a few hours. It was great; I was a new face in town.

Towards the end of the night, I was approached by a CPL from the Mortar Platoon. He started asking me questions then told me, "Fuck off the dance floor." I told him to "Fuck off", and it started getting heated. The members of my platoon said to me, "No, don't fight him, he is Mortars."

He kept looking over then stormed towards me and hit me, but it hardly grazed my face. I fought back, hitting him about five times before he hit the floor.

I was then kicked out of the club. Great start to life in Battalion!

Life in Rifle Company was really not much different to training. We got inspected most days, and if bagged, the good old 2200 hours at guard room still stood. However, our CSM was very keen on PT and appearance, so if you were in good order in the morning and fit, you had quite an easy time. PT would usually be at 0830, and last anything from one to two hours, depending on what the exercise was. After this, there would be admin, if there was nothing else on. However, we were mechanised infantry, so we had the Saxons which were a bag of shit and needed constant attention. This was the driver's responsibility, and he picked his team, so I tried to hide away from that.

Life in the company gradually started to get easier and I was going out socialising a lot with the lads, meeting local girls (naughty me!). What happened on the piss stayed on the piss, as far as we were concerned, and to be honest I really didn't love her anyway. I had rushed into things far too young.

After about six weeks in Aldershot, I couldn't take my wife out because I knew I would bump into one of my other female friends – Aldershot is a small town. There were also times when I would walk through town and spot a girl I knew. She would be with her husband or boyfriend, so we would just walk past without acknowledging each other, then text later on. You see, it worked both ways. It was like a swingers' town… or was that just my perception?

Chapter 34
Thetford Exercise

My first Battalion exercise was in Thetford, and I couldn't believe it was a fucking trench-digging defence/NBC exercise for two weeks. You don't get much worse than that really, whether it's in the winter or the summer. We drove in convoy from Lille Barracks in Aldershot to Thetford in the Saxons, which is the most uncomfortable vehicle on the planet. You feel every bump, it's cramped, and inside it's fucking freezing.

We arrived at the training area and were briefed on what the EX was going to consist of. First, we had to dig the trench. However, this time – surprisingly – the Battalion had brought JCBs to help dig. So, the whole company had the trenches dug and were in routine within 15 hours, as opposed to the three days in training. But then again, we didn't have the luxury of JCBs at ITC.

The EX went on for two phases. At the end of the first one, there was an England football match on, so we got some stand down and went to the HQ where a small TV had been set up and we could have hot dogs and cans of pop. The cans of pop and chocolate were not free; you signed for them and paid on payday. Tight fuckers! England lost, then it was back to the trenches, but with a full night's sleep.

The second phase was at 0500 (Phase 2). The exercise wasn't too bad, to be fair. The biggest lick out was having to take down all defences and re-fill the trenches dug at the end of the Phase 1 exercise.

Once all that was complete, and the drivers had their forced rest, we started our convoy back to Aldershot.

Unfortunately, on the way back to camp there was a road traffic accident on a main public road, involving a Saxon from my platoon (No 5). Sadly, we lost a Corporal in the accident; he was on top cover, and when the Saxon rolled over, he took the full force. It was devastating news, as although I had only known him a short while, he was a lovely guy and a very good soldier. The loss was felt through the Battalion for a long time, and it was a dreadful end to what had been a successful exercise. RIP, mate.

Chapter 35
Life of a Guardsman

As I said before, our normal working day would start at 0800, usually with an inspection. It was then PT every day, then admin. However, with Iraq quickly approaching (date still TBC), we would regularly be out on the area doing fieldcraft training, or we would be on the range doing live firing. If it was on Ashcroft range, it was shit, because it was roughly three miles there and three miles back, so we would always tab there and tab back after the range, getting the PT in as well!

Most nights after work I would go and meet the lads that I had become friends with. Many of them are still close friends to this day, although unfortunately some are no longer with us. I would tell the Mrs, "Only going out for one", then roll in at 3/4am shit-faced, trying to hide the smell of perfume on my clobber.

One night I was out in Yates with a good friend, Sonny, when I had some trouble in the toilet from a Civvy, who must have weighed in at 20 stone, and his skinhead mate. After we left Yates to go to Cheeks, they followed us and attacked us in front of the kebab shop. All I remember really was having a flashback of my childhood! And I do remember he was fucking strong.

I was only 19, and this was a fully grown, 20-stone man! He threw a punch and missed, so I returned the blow, connecting with his jaw. He then grabbed hold of me, but I stepped back and fell down the kerb. I had already put my mouth in his ear, so as I fell down, his ear came off with me. There was a huge fight, with my friend helping. The problem I had when I was there – and younger – was I would black out and be fighting for my life, just as I did as a child at home.

I wish I was able to say this was an isolated incident, but unfortunately it has happened a lot in my life. However, I never have and never will start on an innocent person for no reason; those who do are bullies, in my opinion, and deserve what they get.

Sonny was also married and lived on the same estate as me, and we became good friends and often went out on the booze – ending in drama a lot! I remember one time we were out and had been to a club and pulled a couple of girls. We were walking back towards our pads estate (not sure why, because our wives were home). We were drunk, and there were three lads waiting in the park who knew that the girls were local travelling girls. The lads started kicking off at me and Sonny, so we gave them a few slaps and bugged out, leaving the girls with their cousins or boyfriends – who knows! We were still laughing about it when suddenly a van pulled up, and a bunch of lads with baseball bats jumped out on us. Sonny and I dived in, knocking the first couple to the floor, then we managed to run off through the park, shaking them off.

After the adrenalin had left our bodies, all we could do was laugh about it and congratulate ourselves on the victory, knowing it could have been a very different outcome. We celebrated with a few more hours drinking whiskey at Sonny's house, as we didn't think it was wise to go back into town that evening.

We certainly got up to a lot of shit, but I think I'll leave it there.

Sonny left the Army while I was in Iraq. He had been kept on rear party because he had lost his mother not too long before, and it hit him really hard as they were very close. It was a shame to lose a friend in that way, but I believe he is doing well today, with a family of his own, and no doubt making his mother proud.

Chapter 36
Boxing Team

I joined the Battalion boxing team soon after joining No 2 Company, as it was always a sport I enjoyed – and still do to this day. I would be up and at the boxing gym by 0630am for boxing training three times a week before going on parade at 0800 for roll call. Usually, boxers were exempt from Company PT, but it was not always the case. Some days we would train on an evening, depending on what the boxing coaches had on that day. We never had a ring, though, so we had to make up a square with mats, which wasn't ideal.

There were a few lads in the boxing team that I remember. One guy Antony (who unfortunately was killed in action in Iraq) was a really good boxer, and I enjoyed a few sparring sessions with him.

To this day, I will never forget a three-round sparring session I had with my friend Alfie. He had forgotten his gumshield, so for the whole three rounds I was a human punchbag as I was told I could only defend while he went forwards. I have never forgotten this, and he knows I still owe him ten years later! We laugh about it today as we are both still into our boxing, so maybe we should have a bout!

The problem with boxing for Regiment was that there were always more important things to do, which I understand. So, we never really had a constant boxing team. People would come and go, then come back for a few weeks, then go again. But I tried to go as often as I could.

One evening, our trainer drove five of the better boxers who went training regularly (this included me) to a boxing centre in Brixton. It was one of the gyms where a famous title-winning British boxer started off, I just can't remember which one! The gym was full of boxers training hard and was a real spit-and-sawdust gym, which reminded me of the gym out of *Rocky 3* when he trained with Apollo Creed.

We did some training with them and also some 100 percent sparring, but they were so ring-fit because they were there every day and had been doing it for years. I'm 5.7 in height, but stocky, so I always had to fight guys taller than me with a long jab, which means I always had to go for the body before the head.

At the end of this night, I was fucked and bruised. There was no winner or loser, as it was purely for training, but it was great training and a real eye-opener on how dedicated you need to be if you want to box properly.

We had a few fights scheduled within the next six months, but they were all TBC, due to military operations. And as we knew we would be deploying to Iraq at some point, nothing could be set in stone.

Chapter 37
Driving Course – 1

The company sent me and my friend Colin on a driving course up north, in Leconfield near Hull. We travelled by train, which took us all day to get there, only to be told that the course had been cancelled and we should not have been sent. What a fuck-about that was! However, we managed to blag a night at the camp so that we could go out on the piss in Hull that night. We had a blinding night, both copping off with a couple of northern birds, but at the end of the night, like clockwork, some wanker wanted a fight.

We had just left a club called Waterfronts and were waiting for a taxi when a local lad came over, gobbing off. Colin and I told him to "Fuck off", but he kept coming at us in an aggressive manner. All I did was grab him and push him back, but there is a port there and he was so pissed he fell over the chain and into the water, at about 3am. We had no idea what to do, and the girls were screaming for help. I made a sharp exit and headed back to camp, while Colin fucked off to a girls' house. The guy did get out of the water, I will add.

When we left Hull that day, heading back to Aldershot, we had to have a changeover in a northern town – I can't recall, but I think it was Durham. We had a few hours to wait for the next train, so we found a Yates and got talking to the barmaid. And would you believe it, we missed our fucking train so had to spend the night there on the piss. (What a shame!)

We made it back to camp the next day, and they had no idea the driving course had been cancelled, which was great communication from the Army. We were pissed off, as we could easily have sneaked one more day on the lash somewhere. However, it was Friday, so we had the weekend off anyway. Result.

Chapter 38

My First Tour

OP Telic Confirmed

Number 2 Company were on the Ranges doing our APWT when our Officer commanding the company turned up and told the CSM to form us all up in three ranks ready for a brief. He told us that Number 2 Company would be deploying to Al Basra (Iraq) on OP TELIC – dates TBC, but around back of April/May time – for our Operational training (OPTAG). Training would start shortly, and this gave us around five months before deployment. Most of us were very excited about the news, but there were a few that weren't. It makes me wonder why they were in the Army, let alone the Guards.

Chapter 39
OPTAG Training
(Iraq)

During this training, I moved back into barracks with the lads. OPTAG started very soon after we were told we were definitely being deployed, which also meant that the boxing team had to be disbanded. We needed to train for Iraq, so all our scheduled fights were cancelled, and we returned to our relevant companies full time.

We deployed on a lot of exercise, the worst one being the three-week TEZ EX (this is an exercise where we were all wearing kit that follows everyone and can tell when you have been shot, you have shot the enemy, incoming fire, etc.) on Salisbury Plain. We were issued with lasers on our rifles and sensor jackets, and had halos to put over our helmets. All vehicles also had sensors fitted.

The idea behind the lasers and sensors is that when in contact we would know when we were hit or the vehicle had been destroyed, so we would then have to follow the correct casualty procedure (Cassey vac) and have men missing from platoon until they got replaced, which obviously made our jobs harder. This was the first of many TEZ EX I did. These exercises are broken down into three phases, and every assault/phase is captured on computer by the specialist equipment worn. It shows who has been shot/injured, as well as tactical mistakes, and what has been done properly. At the end of every phase, we would be debriefed on our performance.

By all accounts, we passed our TEZ EX well.

We also did other EXs, such as Riot training (Civ Pop Training), having petrol bombs thrown at us, and people dressed as Arabs giving us shit. Mostly, though, we did lots of live range packages all over the UK, improving our tactics and live firing skills.

OPTAG training went on for around four months, and there were lots of weekdays and weekends spent on exercise preparing for Iraq. But it wasn't constant training, and we still found time to go out some weekends and during the week, when we could get drunk and meet our local girls.

PT had always been a big part of our training, but now that we were being deployed, it was even more important to make sure we were battle fit.

OPTAG also involved hard training in the field, and we had to learn about Improvised Explosive Devices (IEDS) and our Electronic Counter Measures (ECM), so the training was different than what we had been used to doing. At times it could be very boring, particularly if we had to sit through briefs that sometimes went on all day.

I remember one particular Hostile Environment Brief that was held at the boxing gym on Hospital Hill in Aldershot. There must have been around 800 people on the brief, from the lowest-ranking soldier to the highest-ranking officer. A few of us had been out on the pop the night before and were still pissed for half the next day.

The first half of the day was ok because we were still drunk, but we suffered that afternoon with the beer sweats, guys falling asleep, some with beer shits, and we must have stunk of a rotten brewery. After the briefings ended at 1700, it was back to camp, get changed, and back down the town for a beer. That was life in the Army, though. Do your day's work, then go on the piss at night (every night). If you ran out of money by the end of the month, the lads would square you away.

I was having trouble at home which was making life hard for me in Battalion, and I became very snappy with the guys. We had elements of the Mortar Platoon attached to Number 2 Company, and one of the more senior guys, George, had taken notice. One night, I was out in Yates having a drink with a few lads when he approached me and basically started giving me shit. He was a very tall lad and had been in a while, so I just let him have his say; he was pissed anyway. However, as I turned around, he gave me a good right hook to the chin. Luckily, I had a table to lean on and came back with body shots, followed by right hooks to his face. He was bent over the table while I just threw punches, until a few lads got me from behind and held me back. I was told I had to leave, which I thought was bullshit, so I went elsewhere with a thick lip.

I was told by the lads that a Sergeant had actually told George to fill me in but he had come off a lot worse than me, so that plan never worked. In fact, I was told he went into one of the lads' rooms covered in blood and said, "For fuck's sake, that lad is a hard little fucker."

By the time OPTAG was over, it was March 2005, and we were waiting on confirmation of deployment.

Chapter 40
Rigger Marshal Course

After leave, the Battalion deployed halfway through April 2005, but I was left behind as I was placed on a Rigger Marshal Course. This course trains you to bring in helicopters using hand signals, and how to attach and detach under-slung equipment to the helicopter, usually a Chinook or Merlin. The main thing to learn when attaching or detaching under-slung was to earth the static electricity first, or you would get thrown back a long way and receive a hell of a shock.

The course was for one week, then I went back to my unit. I was in the middle of splitting up with my wife at that point, while waiting to find out when my deployment date would be. I was gutted to find out I would not deploy for two weeks, and during that time I was placed on Rear Party, which was doing barrack guard two days on, four days off. Mostly the reason I was upset was due to my home life and what was going on behind closed doors, so I was keen to get away from it!

The week before I was due to deploy, we received the horrifying news that we had lost our first soldier, Antony, who had been killed in action by an IED strike. He was one of the boxers I had sparred with in the boxing team. RIP, Antony.

I had the shit job of looking for his kit back in the UK. Along with two other guys and a welfare officer, we had to go through what would be returned to the stores and, more importantly, what would be sent to his poor family. Doing that really hit home on what I was about to embark on.

Every soldier has to pack up his room and put all personal and military items into MFO boxes, which are then locked away and the key held in the guard room, for situations like this where there is a battlefield casualty or someone is Killed In Action (KIA).

I was given a long weekend off before the Monday that my flight was booked from RAF Brize Norton. On the Monday, my mum came to pick me up. As I was trying to leave, the mother of my daughter went mad as I was trying to say goodbye, pulling her hair out and hitting herself because I was deploying to Iraq, as well as splitting up with her. We do have a child together, but I don't want to mention her in the story as it's not fair on the child. My ex used her as a weapon all the time, and that has only got worse through life! All I will say, though, is that although she treated my daughter as a weapon against me in life, she still looked after her, so I have ultimate respect for that. I never stopped loving my daughter, and I truly hope that one day she and I can have a sit down and a proper chat.

I just told my mum to drive off, and she called my ex's parents to go and make sure my daughter was safe.

It was very early in the morning and my mum dropped me halfway (she was, of course, in tears), while my dad drove me the rest of the way to Aldershot. When I arrived at Battalion, I was expecting to pick up my deserts but was told it was all in Iraq, so I had to deploy to the fucking desert in Combat 95 (green kit). I was, though, given some green combat body armour (with no protection plates) and a helmet, which you need to wear when landing in Iraq.

Along with a few others, I got on the minibus and we made our way to RAF Brize Norton, with me standing out like a bulldog's bollocks in the green kit.

The journey took a few hours, and on arrival we checked in and went through to the departure lounge. After getting over the fact that I had left my daughter and being assured she was safe, I was excited to be going to Iraq, to a war zone. I couldn't wait.

We flew out on a Tri Star RAF plane, which is a very basic, no-thrill flight. When we entered Iraq air space, the captain instructed everyone to put on their CBA and helmet. The descent is nothing like you experience with commercial airlines; it's as if you are nose-diving to the floor.

We had trouble landing as Al Basra airport was under mortar attack, so instead we were diverted to Bahrain and the RAF put us all up in a hotel for 24 hours before trying again. The next evening, we took off and faced more complications landing, due to a sandstorm, but finally we managed to land at Basra International Airport.

Chapter 41
OP TELIC
2005 Tour

It was late April, and I had finally arrived in Iraq. When I got off the plane, the heat hit me instantly. I could not believe how fucking hot it was, and I will never forget the smell – it was like dirt and death. I had arrived a couple of weeks behind the other lads, so I stood out like a sore thumb in my green kit.

Once I got through the Royal Military Police Customs, I recognised a face from HQ Company, and sure enough he was there to meet me and give me my rifle, some ammunition, and bayonet. I asked him about my desert kit, but he said he had no idea.

"Lad, I just have to take you to Shaibah Logistic Base (SLB)," he said, "so you can do your joint reception staging onward movement and integration." (This is known as RSOI.) "Hopefully you will get your kit there."

So, I sat in the back of the snatch, sweating like fuck, with no proper CBA or ballistic helmet. As I was looking out of the rear window, all I could see was blown-up tanks, cars, and trucks; the place was covered in shit, and it stank. But the journey, which took about an hour, passed without any incident.

Shaibah Logistics Base (SLB) was massive, and when we arrived I was immediately shown to my accommodation (a tent with air conditioning) where there were a few other guards on RSOI. I was told I would be picked up in four days, to go to meet my company.

There was still no desert kit for me there – it was with my company – so in the meantime I had to cut around in the scorching heat in combat 95, looking like a wanker, doing my RSOI. The RSOI was a basic range package in the desert, making sure our weapons were zeroed to us, so that whatever I aimed at was correct. We also were given a few briefs on the current threat in Iraq, learned about the biggest threat – the IEDs – and what we had to counter that (our ECM), and how it worked. This was more relevant to people like me (frontline rifle men) because half of the fuckers on the RSOI package probably would never leave their SLB for the six-month tour.

While at SLB, there were a few rocket attacks. But the camp was massive, so unless your accommodation was hit, you hardly knew about it till the Indirect Fire alarms (IDF) went off.

When my RSOI was over, I had a multiple (section of soldiers) come and pick me up in snatches, and they took me to our base, which was the Shatt al-Arab Hotel. On arrival there, I met my OC and CSM, who informed me that there had been a big indirect rocket/mortar attack (this is known as IDF) that night, so the guys had been out on task all night or in hard cover and were now resting. They told me I would re-join 5 Platoon, they welcomed me to Iraq, and I was then finally given all my deserts and shown around.

Shatt al-Arab Hotel had been Saddam Hussein's hotel before Operation Desert Storm, but now it was a big base holding a lot of troops, not just 2 Coy. The building was covered in bullet holes, and you could see the remains of air strike attacks, with parts of the walls in bits. The front of the perimeter had a big concrete wall, as well as Hesco and razor wire on the top, with five made-up sangers with Hesco and sandbags for the troops to keep 24-hour watch (Stags). In the centre of the hotel there was a tower which was always manned, giving 360-degree observation. (This tower was hit directly by a Chinese rocket, luckily not hurting anyone.)

To the rear of the hotel was the Shatt al-Arab River, with an island in the middle, known as Cigar Island. This is where a lot of the IDFs came from to start with. The perimeter of the island was built up with Hesco Bastion and razor wire, but we and a boat unit used it for boat patrols. Everywhere was defended by 24-hour watches by troops. We had a rear gate but hardly used it unless we were going out undercover or in platoon strength, when both gates would be used. Otherwise, we mainly used the front gate (which Sanger 3 covered) overlooking the L-shaped flats – another known area of enemy activity.

Inside the Base we had a cookhouse, so we always had fresh food unless out on operations. There was also a shop run by a little Arab man who travelled 100km every day there and back to sell us DVDs, pop, cigarettes, chocolate, porn, etc. Whatever you wanted, you could request, and he would usually get hold of it for you. He was just making an honest living trying to support his family, but unfortunately later that year he and his family were reported to have been executed by the fuckers (Al Qaida) for working and supplying British Troops.

We also had an internet terminal which we could book into and email family, as well as a phone booth with eight separate phones to use. Every soldier was given a phone card with 20 free minutes a week to call home, and there was the opportunity to top up the minutes if you wanted to. However, if there was an incident with a casualty or KIA, all internet and phone service would be cut out; known as Operation Minimise. This gives the welfare officer of the unit time to notify the soldier's family back home. However, some guys had mobile phones on this tour as well.

Some guys were living inside the hotel itself, but most were in tents outside or container units. 5 Platoon were in the containers, which were made for living in and had air conditioning, so it wasn't too bad unless a mortar landed in the area, which would rip straight through the container.

I was sharing with three Mortar lads attached to 5 Platoon, and one of them was G who I'd had a fight with in Yates a few months before. I asked him for a chat on our own, and we shook hands and became good friends.

I met my Platoon Sergeant, who told me that 2 Company had three rotations, which 5/6/7 Platoon rotated through. This was split up into four night patrols, four days of guarding the camp on the sangers or the tower, and four day patrols.

Chapter 42

Al Basra

First off, let me say that Basra in 2005 was a total shithole, mired in poverty and corruption. The city had been very built-up with buildings, residential communities and villages, but so many of the buildings were blown up and left destroyed during Desert Storm, leaving people living on the streets. The whole city had a distinct smell of death and garbage, and it's something I have never forgotten. There was rubbish everywhere, with stray dogs roaming the place and rats the size of Jack Russells – I shit you not!

In some areas there was no sewer system, so people's shit and piss would just be tossed in a river or down an alley. You would always be harassed for money and water – usually it was kids who were sent over to approach us, and they were stinking and covered in flies. Back then, I wasn't that much of an emotional person, but sometimes they got lucky, depending on the situation and what was going on at the time on the ground.

There was a well-known market, called "Five-Mile Market" which was basically a fucking huge dirty market on the side of a main road. And the one thing anyone will tell you who had been down there in the day, was the awful smell of shit and fish. The fish market must have stretched out for 100 metres, with the fish just lying on the floor, covered in flies, in the scorching summer Iraq heat. You can never forget a smell like that.

After patrolling down there a few times, it was also normal to see shepherds in the middle of the street cutting off the heads of sheep they had sold, and throwing the heads into the back of a truck (not the sort of thing you see in London). It was also normal to see people who were clearly knocking on Heaven's door just lying on the ground in a shit state, with no help, along with the odd corpse rotting in the gutter.

Chapter 43

My First Night Patrol With 10B

On my first night, 5 Platoon had rotated to night patrols, which meant I would be out on patrol that evening. I had my weapon and bayonet already, my deserts, and my combat CBA with plates and ballistic helmet. I was also issued with a Light Laser Monocle (LLM), which is a bit of night vision that goes onto your helmet. The laser was attached to our weapons, so could be used either as a red laser or infrared, so you could only see what the laser was pointing at when you were wearing the Monocle. It was a good bit of kit and fairly new at the time. I was also issued with a CWS, to be attached to SA80 for night vision, along with additional ammunition and mags, two high explosive grenades, and a Smoke Foss grenade.

So, I sorted my bed space and kit out, then got some rest. Before patrol, we would have a pre-intelligence brief, with a debrief after a patrol. (The only time we never had a pre-int brief was if we were crashed out due to an incident – something which happened a lot over six months.)

On my int brief that first night, we were told that some of the local population had informed us of suspicious activity, and our guys on guard had heard bursts of gunfire and tracers coming from around the same area – the dockyard and old train track. It was believed that an IDF attack the previous night had also come from around the same area. So, we were tasked to go and investigate what was going on. If we were contacted, we should engage the enemy; if not, we were simply showing that we had guys on the ground and dominating our area of responsibility (AOR).

Before every patrol, every man drank a bottle of water and made sure we had our camomile packs full of water. We prepped our weapons for firing, made sure all ECM was working, and that we had spare batteries. Then we all made sure we could talk through our personal role radio, with the Commanders carrying out full radio checks.

The drivers had the responsibility of first parading the snatches, making sure they were operational. To be honest, snatches were a bag of shit and at best would only stop a 5.56 round penetrating the armour – if we were lucky; a 7.62 round at the most. But any high calibre round would penetrate the snatch, while an IED would destroy it – and probably a few of the guys inside.

On patrol we always took along an interpreter who was from elsewhere in Iraq, so that locals would not recognise him. This was to avoid putting him and his family in danger of execution.

I was briefed on our standard operation procedures at Vulnerable Points (VPs), which meant we would stop short, do our five- and 20-metre checks for IEDs, then walk vehicles through the VP. At any point that we dismounted the vehicles, we would always do our five- and 20-metre checks with cover provided by top cover on the snatches. As time went on, I usually did top cover, which was something I quite enjoyed.

All vehicles carrying ECM kept a distance between them. This was to extend the coverage of the ECM bubble, giving us protection from IEDS. But the ECM would not stop a command wire or an Explosively Formed Projectile (EFP).

The EFP was not in operation until halfway through our tour – something I will go onto later. If there were any vehicles without ECM, it would be placed in the middle of the convoy so that it still had ECM protection.

With regards to ECM, there were three separate devices we used. One was very heavy, called the Chub, and we also used the Axenth & Baltimore – all equipment which was able to be man-packed.

Not all our patrols involved vehicles, as many were on foot, but we still had to man-pack the ECM and carry it. And believe me, you did not want the Chub. It was a really heavy bit of kit to add to all the other gear we had to take.

As we left base that night on my first patrol, I had mixed emotions of excitement and slight nerves. We had been given a few tasks to do and places of interest to investigate, and sometimes we heard gunfire, though it was not direct. Then we received reports from the sangers that they had seen tracer rounds. They gave us the rough direction, so we mounted the snatches and went to investigate. The problem is that the terrorists used this sometimes as a come-on, so that when troops went to investigate, they were ambushed by IED strikes, sometimes followed up by a gunman.

On that occasion, we found nothing, and my first patrol ended without incident. Getting the first one under my belt made me feel more confident, and I knew somehow that I wouldn't buckle under pressure when shit hit the fan. After the patrol, it was into routine sleeping and getting up for meals. Some lads went to the gym – I was one of them – while most just sunbathed (OP BRONZE).

We had a few IDF attacks on the base during my first days there, but they were mostly rockets or mortar attacks. The first time was the morning after the second night patrol, so I was asleep and woke up to loud explosions going off and horns sounding (IDF alarms). Me and the three other guys woke up in a daze, half naked, and quickly put on our CBA and helmets. The SOP was to run to hard cover, or get under the bed and make yourself as small a target as possible until you could reach hard cover. So, we ran in boxers and flip-flops, with CBA and helmets on, to hard cover some 20 metres or so away.

The day patrols and QRF (HQ) got crashed out to try and counter the attack. But the problem was that often by the time we deployed out on the ground, all we would find would be a possible fire position. It really was a game of cat and mouse and could be very frustrating.

We spent our four night patrols in snatches, going to known areas of insurgency to look for trouble, but everything was as it should be. And when my first rotation of night patrols finished, it was on to Sanger bashing (guard duty).

Chapter 44
Sanger Bashing and Tower Watch

Sangers are basically man-made watch towers made with sand which is filled in HESCO. There were five sangers, so we did a rotation of eight hours on guard, eight hours off, and we rotated around the sangers every two hours. It was hard work, and in daylight it would be one man in each sanger – except Sanger Three where there always two men, because it was the main gate and principal threat for suicide bombers. We also had two men behind the front gate checking Locally Employed Civilians (LECs), both on the way in and out of base. They would often try to steal things before they left, but the most important time was when they reported for work, when they needed a full body search and their ID checked. We would have the shit truck in every day to empty the porter toilets, and escorting this truck around was a honking job, due to the smell.

At night guard, it was stepped up to having two men in each sanger. In each one there was a good range of night vision – the best being a device that picks up on heat sources. Its only problem was that it made a fucking loud noise, but it had a good focus range, and you could easily make out people and objects in the pitch black. The tower also had other good night vision, and there was always a hidden

RECCE platoon in an OP hidden in the tower, feeding us back information.

We doubled up at night for the sake of night vision and rotating round the sangers, which helped you stay alert, plus you had someone to talk to. Eight hours on stag at night is hard work. Guys who were caught sleeping on stag were either lucky and got a kicking from the Guard Commander, or unlucky and put on report. That meant going on OC orders, and the going rate was a month's wages taken from you. I know of one guy who was caught three times and ended up being sent to military prison in Colchester (Glasshouse) for the rest of the tour.

On the guard rotation, everyone wanted tower duty, as this was four hours on with eight hours off – much better than guard duty. After my first rotation of guard, I was pretty fucked, and it was then onto day patrols to see the real Al Basra in the summer heat.

On day patrols we never went out and came back at the same time every day. We tried not to set a pattern of life so that the enemy would not find it easy to target us. Some days we would have set tasks like going to local police stations and villages, trying to gather information, doing a bit of hearts and minds. But the problem was that Iraq was so corrupt at that time, and people would just tell you what you wanted to hear then report back to the enemy. In fact, by the end of tour we were pretty sure that some of the Iraq police were corrupt and that they had arranged and helped with attacks on us.

The other problem with Iraq in 2005 was that Saddam Hussein was on the run and there was no law or order in the country, so the Sunni and Shia tribes were constantly fighting each other for power. We would get called out to an incident where they would be having a firefight, but as soon as we arrived, they turned their guns on us and fought together. What a load of shit!

On some patrols, both day and nights, the people could go from being very hospitable to the next day being the shitheads throwing bricks at us in the same area, or responsible for IED strikes. We never knew what to expect.

IEDs were going off all over Al Basra at this point, so at every Vulnerable Point (VP) we would stop short and walk all vehicles through the VP, checking for signs of disturbance to the ground for a hidden IED or a hidden command wire leading to an enemy waiting to blow us up. After a while we knew what to look for, as there are signs when some shit is about to hit the fan. But I will come onto that.

Chapter 45
Main Incidents

After around a month, things started growing more hostile out on the ground, mostly with homemade IEDs taking out a lot of our vehicles and causing casualties and KIAs. It seemed that quite a lot of the IEDs were aimed at the close protection contractors.

At that stage, an IED had yet to penetrate a Challenger 2 tank, although they had been able to make an IED strong enough to take out a Warrior. All the shit from up north in Baghdad seemed to be on its way down to us, and we came under heavy IDF a few times a week – sometimes a few times a day – then things would go quiet for a week. Certainly, getting some heavy IDF a few times a week kept us on our toes!

IEDS were also being found all over the place. In fact, one went off on a 6 Platoon day patrol, on the bridge crossing the Shatt al-Arab River. But the terrorists had messed it up and placed it too far under the bridge, so all it did was cause a big bang and a hole in the concrete. It was so fucking lucky, because if it had been placed slightly differently, we would have been talking about plenty of casualties and possibly KIAs.

Night-time, hard knock

It came down from the top that there was going to be an operation with 2 Company very soon, using gathered intelligence. It was only a rumour to start with, but then all of 2 Company was stood down, and the Royal Artillery came from SLB to take over all guard duties for 48 hours.

We were given a brief by our OC (Major) that we would be conducting a deliberate hard knock on a house where it was suspected they were making IEDs. We had a couple of RMPs attached for POW handling, but the OP was very secret and that's why we only got 48 hours' notice. Once we were briefed in full, we did a rehearsal inside our base the night before.

On the day of the operation, we all knew what our relevant tasks would be. 5 Platoon would be the first on the scene; half of 10A would cordon off the area and do five- and 20-metre checks for IEDs; the break-in platoon was 10B 5 (the multiple I was in); 7 Platoon would clear the house; and 6 would do the search operation. However, on operations things can and do take an unexpected twist, so we all had to be prepared for situations like an ambush with IEDs and/ or a shooter, women and children willing to fight/or being used as human shields. Literally anything. Finally, we were all prepped, and headed off to get some rest before our night operation.

At 0100 we were ready to go. We had a kit check and made sure we had all operational equipment we needed, both to carry out the task with success, and to extract if it was failed or compromised. We were all very confident and ready to go.

We also carried additional items, such as blacked-out goggles and plastic cuffs for potential Prisoners of War (POW). The use of sandbags over heads was no longer allowed, but we had them in case. And of course, we had two interpreters to give our commands to the locals and, more importantly, our targets.

All vehicles were in order of march, with 5 Platoon leading the company with two snatches, with 10A at the front to do the cordon; the other half of 5 Platoon (20B) was the next two snatches for the start of the deliberate OP – the break-in phase. All other vehicles were behind us, in accordance with their part in the operation.

We left Base at 0130hrs, as the start of the OP was due to take place at 0200 – two hours before the locals got up for morning prayers. The aim was to catch them off guard, when things were quiet.

We all left in convoy, using no lights, just night vision with LLM (night vision). The target house was not far – maybe 10k away – but we still had to be ready for an ambush or IED strike on the way, as the intelligence could have been false and used as a come-on for an ambush.

10A were first on scene, and they went in without any incident. 20B then went in with force. Lights went on in the target building, and I noticed three Arabs sleeping on the roof. I pointed my weapon and shouted at them, but they seemed dazed and had no idea what was going on. I then called for the interpreter to shout commands at them. While all this was going on, other members of the Platoon had kicked the door in, and 6 & 7 were in the target's house doing their job.

Once the three Arabs had been searched, they were sent downstairs, and one or two others were tasked to re-search them, handcuff them with plastic cuffs, blindfold them with blacked-out goggles, then separate them, on their knees with heads facing the wall and hands behind their back. They were gobbing off and not co-operating, so we had to be forceful with them. We told the interpreter to tell them to shut up and stop communicating with each other.

We could hear an Arab woman screaming as she was being led out by an RMP. She was shouting in Arabic to the arrested men and trying to go to them, but I stopped her and led her to a female RMP who dealt with her and led her away. The whole op lasted about 45 minutes, during which time the search team found evidence of bomb-making material. So, the Arabs I was guarding were arrested and put in a snatch for extraction back to camp.

The convoy then began in opposite order, with 5 Platoon last off the scene. No shots were fired, we had gone in and done our job, and were out before sunrise. It had been a very professional operation, and the great feedback we received on the debrief gave us all a sense of achievement.

IED Strike

5 Platoon were on day patrols when we were crashed out to an IED strike, which was in our area of responsibility. Although we were first on the scene, we could not go rushing in because there could have been a follow-up shoot or other IEDs waiting for us. Once the QRF had been on scene a few minutes, we did five- and 20-metre checks, then extended the cordon so there was a safe distance and all-round defence. However, there was a suspicious package seen about 50 metres from the original IED strike (it was, in fact, an IED). The call sign hit was not from our regiment, but a Multiple from the Royal Artillery doing what was meant to be a simple task to the Shatt al-Arab Hotel and then back to SLB. It was a route that we used regularly, and we had actually been past the same spot hours before this IED strike. (It only takes the enemy minutes to set up an IED.)

On that particular incident, we were there for hours. We had to wait because there was another IED found, and Explosive Ordnance Disposal specialists were tasked to come out and disarm the device. We also had news reporters flying in with helicopters.

When all the hype calmed down and it was confirmed safe to leave the area (you know this when all the locals start appearing again), we all moved back to base along with the blown-up snatch.

We knew it wasn't going to be a pleasant debrief, and we were right. One of the guys in the snatch had sustained critical injuries, and the Commander had been killed at the scene. It was mentioned that, looking at the evidence, it had been an IED strike, possibly followed up with a shoot. What was even more disturbing was when we got told that the soldier who had been killed had his wedding ring missing, and it was nowhere to be seen at the scene of the IED strike. This meant some fucker had stolen his wedding ring while he lay there dying. I can't believe how sick some people are, and I only have sympathy for his wife and family. I believe the soldier who was critically injured was flown back to Birmingham hospital, and his life was saved.

We were called out to a number of IED strikes over six months. One other that sticks in my mind was an IED strike on a convoy of American armed CP contractors. Their two 4x4s were totally destroyed on the main supply route (MSR), and there were no survivors of the attack. It was not a pleasant scene, and all we could do was our usual SOPs five- and 20-metre checks and cordon off the scene until the vehicles and bodies were recovered.

20B Night Contact

In 5 Platoon, when we were on night patrols it was everyone's best rotation, because it was not as hot, and it was quieter.

One night we were tasked to go round doing snap vehicle checkpoints, checking people's ID through the interpreter, and making random visits to local police stations. We had been out on patrol for a few hours and had carried out a few tasks when we stopped around 300 metres away from an Iraqi Police compound, which was in a very built-up area. We planned to be there no more than 15-20 minutes to carry out snap VCPs.

We dismounted, leaving one guy on each snatch as top cover, and made our five- and 20-metre checks, then set up the VCP. After about ten minutes, we heard a car travelling at speed but could not see the vehicle anywhere. We then heard the sound of gunfire and the thud and crack of the rounds.

They were coming from what seemed to be all directions, hitting our snatches and the road and buildings on either side of us.

I hit the deck, trying to find cover and look for a fire point to return fire (RTR), but I could not see fuck all to shoot. Under Card Alpha, you can only fire if you can positively ID the enemy, or if you see a human life is at risk from someone else. In other words, you can't just start firing at suspected positions, which in my opinion is a pretty shit rule.

The gunfire only lasted for a few minutes then all went quiet. Amazingly, not one soldier was hit, nor did we manage to fire back at the fuckers. But it all happened so quickly, and by the time we found cover and tried to identify a shooter, it was over.

The local police were in and around the buildings afterwards, asking us what had happened, and thinking they were the target of a terrorist attack. Personally, I think it was total bullshit, and it was those corrupt fuckers all along. They just didn't like to have a proper firefight, but would shoot and scoot, then make out they were your friends again. But that's my opinion. Also, they knew our Rules of Engagement and so did the terrorists, and they used it to their advantage.

In the debrief we all got a well done from the CSM and Section Commander for staying calm and professional. It had been logged as an official enemy contact, but it was just very annoying that we couldn't shoot the fuckers back!

Chapter 46
Suspicious Vehicles Around Area of Mortar Attack on Our Base

We had a nice wake-up call with a big IDF strike during the night. Mortars were landing inside the camp; some went off, some never and were cordoned off for the EOD to disarm the mortar. After every mortar attack we had a soak-in period just to make sure the attack was over and to account for possible casualties, then we would do OP wide awake. This is where we would all go round looking for damage and unexploded ordinates. One rocket had gone through the wall of the hotel near where a soldier was in his bed asleep. Somehow, he was not seriously injured, but he was sent home as it burst his eardrums.

That day there was a rocket found facing our camp, and a suspicious vehicle spotted by our intelligence, so EOD went out with another call sign to disarm the rocket. As we were on day patrols, we were sent to try and identify the vehicle spotted around the area. Everyone else at base was in hard cover, as the rocket could have been set off at any time.

I was not on top cover, but Mac spotted a vehicle with two Arabs acting strangely. As we approached them, they tried to speed off, so we gave chase, cutting them with our two snatches. I was straight out of the back and, without thinking, opened the driver's side door and physically dragged him out of the car. I made him lie in the sand face down and had my rifle pointed at his head, and I told my friend to do the same with the passenger. Anger had taken over for me, and I was pissed off. Luckily for them I was not the Commander.

Our Section Commander got the interpreter to talk to them and we searched their vehicle. We did find weapons, but they had permits for them, so we had no choice but to let the fuckers go. I was told afterwards, "Fucking hell, be careful what you do in front of people. However, good drills, good to see."

Chapter 47

Contact at the Mortar Pit Inside Camp

As we had elements of Mortars attached to us, one night the Sergeant from my room, Sgt G (he was Mortars), took us to see what the 81mm mortar was all about. He let us drop a few illume bombs down the barrel as an interest period and a bit of a recruitment for after the tour.

We were there for maybe an hour and had fired a few illume bombs when all off a sudden we heard rapid gunfire; the rounds were coming straight over our heads and hitting the sand and the containers behind us. We all dropped to our belt buckles, trying to find cover behind sandbags while the rounds were landing all round us. This went on for a few minutes and there was even a sanger in front of us, but they said they could not see a firing point.

When it finished, we all had a Re-Org and checked each other for injuries before we all burst out laughing at what had been another unbelievable near miss. The Mortar Platoon went straight into an illume fire mission to try and expose the enemy. There was a big electric factory next to camp, so we came to the conclusion that some fucker must have been on the rooftop shooting down at us, once again with no rounds returned, and – unbelievably – no-one was hit! We all started to feel like target practice for the fuckers. Good job they were a shit shot!

Ambush

There was a big bridge separating our AOR, and on the other side of the bridge was the Danish AOR. Our side was meant to have a 24-hour manned checkpoint, staffed by the Iraq Police. But it never was. It was a place we would visit frequently, as it was on the Main Supply Route (MSR) and had a route to SLB before crossing the bridge.

Without binoculars, the guys on Sanger 3 could just about see the bridge. With binoculars, you could clearly see the MSR and bridge, but not what people were doing there.

We were once again on day patrols when a call came in stating that there was an attack going on at the checkpoint on the MSR. However, Sanger 3 had not heard any kind of contact from that area. Our OC tasked both 10A & 10B of 5 Platoon to go and investigate, with extreme caution.

We had to pass through a lot of VPs to get there, and the area was very quiet with not a person in sight. This gave us cause for concern, and we were now certain it could be an ambush. The commanders decided to go a different way to confuse the enemy if it was an ambush. Not keeping a pattern of life and a same routine is vital when operating against enemy like this. When we had the target checkpoint in sight, we dismounted. Leaving one guy on top cover on each snatch, we then slowly and tactically moved towards the checkpoint, always stopping short at selected RVs, always doing five- and 20-metre checks.

When we were roughly 1000 metres from the checkpoint, there was no sign of anyone there. In fact, there was nobody in sight, and even local traffic on a main MSR seemed quiet. This was either a big come-on and they had something waiting for us, or it was a big hoax. So, we slowly advanced, all sweating like pigs and adrenalin pumping, waiting for what might come next.

As we got about 800 metres from the checkpoint, we heard an explosion and rapid machine gun fire. We all dropped down and looked for the fire point, but we could tell that the rounds were not coming in our direction, so we started to advance towards the checkpoint in fire teams. A different call sign from a mixed multiple from SLB reported the contact, but the IEDs had not hit their snatches and there were no casualties reported, so they drove through the ambush. We were told to wait and stand by for a counterattack. Once the contacted call sign was out of the way and safe, we moved in. Expecting a fight, we had warrior QRF crashed out that stormed in first with their armour, with us following on.

When we got to the checkpoint there was no-one there or any evidence of a firefight, but 100 metres into the desert we found a fire position with an abandoned rocket-propelled grenade case and brass from fired rounds. There was also a command wire found with an exploded IED.

Basically, what had happened was that the enemy had called it in at the Shatt al-Arab, expecting us to rush to the scene. But they had seen the other convoy first, so panicked and changed their attack onto them, not us. Had they ignored the other patrol, let it pass and waited for us, we would have walked into a heavy ambush, because they would have had us were they wanted us. It had also been a good call for us to go in from a different direction on the hunch that it was a set-up, and to go in slowly and fully tactical. I'm sure that all this and the fact that the enemy messed it up saved some of 5 Platoon from serious injury or KIA. The multiple that was ambushed did not suffer any casualties whatsoever, thankfully.

Had that multiple not been tasked that day and gone past that spot at the exact time, it would have had a different ending for sure.

Hearts and Minds Operations

We also had some hearts and minds tasks over the six-month tour, when we would visit local schools, hospitals, orphanages, that type of thing. Our job as troops was to escort the hearts and minds officers to the location, do our five- and 20-metre checks, then cordon off and guard the area while the officers did their charity thing, giving away clothes and water to the kids. This soft approach was a good way of gaining trust and getting information from local people, but personally I found it boring, and it could go on all day. I prefer the hard approach!

Chapter 48

Sanger 3 Shoot

5 Platoon's rotation was Guard at this point. We were briefed the day ahead to expect Arabs coming into camp, as they were reporters for a hearts and minds campaign. The reporters would have been informed of the correct procedure on entering, plus there was a warning sign – in both English and Arabic – on the first concrete block outside the camp, saying: NO UNAUTHORISED VEHICLES BEYOND THIS POINT. YOUR LIFE MAY BE AT RISK IF YOU PASS THIS POINT! After this sign, there was a separate searching bay where all people and vehicles were searched before entering camp.

We were also briefed that as we would be having reporters in on this particular day, the vehicle-based IED (VBIED – suicide bomber) threat had also gone up. It was certain that the enemy would have heard reporters were visiting, so they could use this as an opportunity to attack using a VBIED.

I started on Sanger 2 then moved to Sanger 3, where I was with another guy that we called Dicko. I had two hours in this sanger, and Dicko was on his final hour. He was one of the more senior and experienced GDSM and had done a tour of Northern Ireland. We were both in helmets, as sometimes there would be sniper shots from the L-shaped flats about 600 metres to the front of Sanger 3. As usual, they would only take a pot shot, so there was never any chance of identifying and shooting the fuckers.

The pair of us were having a chat, watching our arcs that we were more than familiar with, when I saw a red car travelling down the road from the left. It had passed Sanger 2 towards camp, although this didn't mean it would turn right and come into camp, as there a number of other ways it could turn. However, suddenly and without warning it turned right and drove past the warning sign and towards the front gate.

I fired one warning shot at the vehicle and it came to an abrupt stop. I shouted at the Arab to get out of his car, as well as using hand signals. And as he got out, I shouted at him to lie on the fucking floor! The Guard Commander came up to the sanger, saw what had happened, and sent out the searchers. It turned out that this guy was a reporter – just an ignorant Arab who chose not to read the sign. I got a pat on the back and a well done, but my heart was beating so quickly and my adrenalin was pumping. It was the first shot fired in anger from the sanger.

Dicko was then relieved by another guy named Mr C. We had a chat while still observing our arcs, and it could only have been 20 or 30 minutes later when I spotted a white, flat-bedded truck with three Arabs coming the same way as the last vehicle… but at greater speed. I said to Mr C, "No fucking way!" but he just looked at me and shrugged his shoulders.

The truck turned right and drove straight past the warning sign, so I immediately fired a warning shot at the vehicle. But instead of it stopping, it accelerated towards the front gate. I then took aim and fired a shot directly through the windscreen at the driver's head. The round went straight through the windscreen, and the truck came to a stop. I grabbed Mr C and pulled him to the floor of the sanger, waiting for an explosion, and at the same time sent a situation report (SIT REP) to the guard room. All this took seconds, but it felt like a lifetime.

I then thought about the other two Arabs in the vehicle and whether they could detonate the device, so I got up with the intention of shooting them. But as I got up and looked, the other two guys were out of the truck, lying on the floor, and I think praying to Allah. It was all very confusing, and every fucker was trying to talk on the radio.

After a few minutes, the same Guard Commander came up and said, "What the fuck's going on?" I was trying to catch my breath and explain, when he saw the vehicle with the bullet hole and the driver slumped behind the windscreen with a hole in the front of his head. The two passengers were still on the ground outside the truck. As Mr C was in the sanger, the CSM and OC (Company Commander) both came to see what had happened. The CSM said to me, "Having fun today, lad?" I was then relieved of duties for some time out, and the QRF and the medics went out with the RMPs to investigate what had happened.

My OC and CSM congratulated me and said, "You have done the right thing; others would have bottled it. You have demonstrated completely how a professional soldier should act in that situation. You have our full support if there is an investigation."

I didn't know what to do with myself after this happened. I went to the NAAFI and bought a chocolate bar and can of pop, and even though I don't smoke, I bought ten cigarettes. Then I went back to my accommodation, listened to some music from Keane, sat in the sun, and smoked my first fag.

Later that day, I was called to see the RMPs to give my version of what had happened. They told me they had taken statements off everyone concerned, and there was going to be no further action taken on this incident because I had followed the correct procedures of Card Alpha – which covers the rules of engagement. It turned out that the Arabs in the truck were not suicide bombers, but news reporters from Saudi Arabia. The driver had just panicked at the warning shot and put his foot on the accelerator instead of the brake.

The next day on the daily orders, my Officer in Command congratulated me and said he had put me up for a recommendation. This means some sort of military appraisal, more than likely a Mention in Dispatches, which is a certificate one below a medal. I am certainly not suggesting this act should have been worthy of medal.

Things were going really well for me, and I had also crossed that line where I'd had to decide whether or not to use lethal force. It's different if someone is shooting at you, but in a situation like that you have to act on instinct, and training should kick in. It was an event that changed my life and one I will never forget. However, I do not regret it at all, and I can live with my decisions during that incident. That day I decided to start smoking to try and calm me down, as there was no alcohol. So, I smoked two, and the same the next day, then I stopped smoking altogether. I hated the smell on my hands and clothes, so I gave the rest of the fags to the lads and have not touched one since.

After that, I was always asked to escort the Platoon Commander when going into police stations, and I was always on top cover (my choice). I had a really itchy trigger finger and was always looking for a fight. The saying is that the first time is always the hardest; it gets a lot easier after you cross that line and can start to enjoy it, and want a fight or excuse to shoot some fucker. To this day, I still feel the same but have just learnt how to deal with it.

However, that incident with everything leading up to it in Iraq and at home as a child, was the start of PTSD... I just didn't know it yet.

Chapter 49

Kuwait

I was given a 24-hour stand down because of my Recommendation for my actions in the sanger on that day I used lethal force, and I got to go to Kuwait with some other lads. We had to drive there in our snatches, which took about four hours, and all the way to the border we had to be fully tactical. We were ambushed by an angry mob of Arabs as we were passing through one small village, but only had big rocks thrown at us. We just drove through the village, as even a snatch can withstand a rock! As soon as we hit the border, the security was of course very tight, but I'm sure they knew we were coming.

Once we passed through the security border and into Kuwait, we all had to dismount our snatches, unload our weapons, turn ECM off, and remove body CBA and helmets, as this is a sign that we were not there for aggression. We were more than happy to, because it gave us a break. It was strange that you literally passed one border line and you were safe; step the other side, and you needed to be ready for combat.

Driving through Kuwait, we all took it in turns to look through top cover, and it was clear it was a very rich country. We eventually got to the American camp where we were having our stand down. It was only for one night, but that was better than fuck all.

Their camp was huge, with a big swimming pool, a cinema, and an amazing all-you-can-eat cookhouse. There was literally every type of food going, and also a row of six-foot fridges filled with pop, energy drinks, and fruit juice. Everything was free and top of the range! I mean, for fuck's sake, we felt lucky at the Shatt al-Arab that we had a pizza shop and a small NAAFI. Their shopping mall PX was huge, and it sold everything. You could even buy a Harley Davidson! I mean, come on. There was also live entertainment, and the Yanks were giving it their typical loudness.

We had left Iraq at night to make the most of the stand down, so we had time to arrange a trip into the local city. Wearing civilian clothes, but carrying our MOD90 and passport, we walked round in a group trying to find somewhere to have an alcoholic drink. But Kuwait is totally dry, and alcohol is viewed in the same way as a class A drug is in the UK.

We walked through the indoor shopping centre, which was incredibly clean. And we also found the beach, strolling around in just our shorts, messing about in the water. To start with, there were a few locals on the beach – the women all in burkas – but as soon as we went on the sand, everyone left. Thinking back, it was because we had our tops off and they find that offensive. Also, they don't really like us!

At one point, on a different stand down, one of the lads needed a piss and was in the indoor shopping centre. He went into what looked like a toilet where a man would piss. Noticing there were flip flops outside, he took his shoes off to respect their rules, and he took a piss in the fountain with running water, which does look like a regular toilet in the UK. However, it caused a huge problem because it turned out he was in a place for prayers, not a toilet. Luckily, after some explaining and apologies, he left the shopping centre with nothing more said.

I spent the night I had off next to the pool, chatting to different people. I got talking to a girl I was sure I recognised, and it turned out she was a medic based in Aldershot. I can't recall why she was there. I also got my hands on a bottle of vodka from another soldier. I paid over the odds, but it was worth it, and we all drank it and had a laugh. It was just good to chill out. The next morning, we visited the cookhouse one last time, stuffing our faces and filling our pockets full of free pop and energy drinks that we would have had to pay for back at our camp. Then we made our way back to Iraq again, stopping at the border this time to load up and put all CFO on and ECM before heading back to the Shatt al-Arab.

Back Into Routine

After the stand down, it was back into normal routine, although I had my rest and recuperation (RNR) coming up. I was on the last RNR rotation. RNR is when you are flown home to the UK for two weeks' leave, then you would report back to your unit in the UK, be driven to RAF Brize Norton, and flown back to Iraq to finish your tour. However, until I was on that plane, my mind was firmly focussed on the job.

We kept on getting mortar attacks, but by that point we just used to laugh about them and stroll to hard cover. It had become second nature by that stage.

One afternoon, when my rotation was nights, I borrowed George's iPod and sat on the top of the Shatt roof a bit for Op Bronze (sunbathing for my RNR). I went to the top of the hotel, on the roof, which was the best spot. However, I forgot to put on my door where I was going, which was an SOP, I fell asleep with his iPod on full blast for three hours, and forgot to take my dog tags off.

When I eventually went back to my accommodation, as red as a lobster, people were asking me, "Ben, where the fuck have you been?" Apparently, there had been a mortar alarm sounded, as there was a rocket fired at camp. But I had been knocked out in the sun with music blaring and had heard fuck all. I got a right bollocking for this, and was given a punishment of filling 100 sandbags. Fair enough, I took it on the chin, but I was more concerned about my sunburn and the perfect markings where my dog tags had been. I was in pain for at least a week while the skin peeled off.

Sanger Contact

I was on night guard and took over Sanger 1, where I was on stag with a new lad – a guy I am still friends with today, and I'm actually godfather to one of his beautiful daughters. We were chatting and he said he had a mobile phone. I asked if I could use it, and he let me, so I called my family and friends (I think he is still paying off the bill today!).

All of a sudden, heavy machine gun fire was aimed at Sanger 2, and the tracer rounds were also coming over our sanger. I put up three boxes of chamomiles, as I could see the fire point. Sanger 2 was asking for permission to return fire, but I was shouting down the radio, "For fuck's sake, under Card Alpha you can return fire!"

I carried on putting the chamomiles over the fire position, but I was dying to get into the sanger that was under contact. I could not fire from my sanger, as the enemy contact was not in my arcs of fire, and it would have meant firing too close to the sanger that was in contact, putting our lads in danger. I could also not just abandon my post and run off to the sanger in contact.

I was trying to ask for permission to go to the other sanger, but the radio was full of people sending situation reports, known as SITREPS. This went on for a good 15 minutes, and then a Land Rover pulled up and someone shouted for me to get in and assist in the sanger under contact. They drove me to it, but by the time I was in the sanger, the firing had stopped and QRF had been crashed out. So that was the end of that.

I said to the guy on stag, "What's your problem, you morons? Why didn't you return fire?" They both said they had been waiting for permission to fire from the Ops Room.

If I had been their Section Commander, I would have kicked the shit out of them! It is a perfect example of the decision I made on Sanger 3, when I had fired two warning shots at two vehicles, and used a direct shot at one of the drivers. If these same two lads had been in my sanger that day, the chances are the truck would have been loaded with a 1000lb bomb and, by bottling it, people would have been killed. It's just sod's law.

So, rotations carried on. Due to RNR, there were always people away, so we all mucked in to fill the gaps, even if that meant an extra guard duty or patrol with a different platoon. Hence the reason I had been on guard that particular night.

Chapter 50

Company Effort
Night Foot Patrol

D ue to a rise in IED attacks, reports of enemy activity by local civilians, as well as 3 Company getting a hiding with IEDs and IDF at the Old State Buildings (OSB) in the centre of Basra - also in our AOR - the Company Commander of both 2 and 3 Company decided that we would conduct a show of force on foot.

This patrol would dominate a lot of ground and let the enemy know we were there, making it harder for them to conduct their operations.

2200 hours

Some left on foot out of camp, others were dropped off by snatches. We were on foot but we also had Warriors patrolling all the main roads. It was a proper show of force, and at the time we left camp there were plenty of people going about their business.

As we patrolled past a local police station, I noticed a police officer with his weapon in a fire position. I shouted to my commander and pointed my weapon at him, using the red laser on the LLM. I was ready for him to make one move and I would have dropped him. The interpreter was called, and everything was sorted by word of mouth. Apparently, we scared him, but I have my own thoughts on this.

We moved through our AOR, going through the five-mile market and places we would be seen. Even though it was at night, our presence was noticed. We patrolled around and through little residential areas, and we also made unannounced visits to some of the local police stations. Throughout the patrol we would take turns carrying the ECM, as it's fucking heavy along with everything else. The other problem with ECM is that it sends out a silent frequency which a human cannot hear but which drives the dogs fucking crazy. They gave our position away before anything else, and sometimes the dogs would attack us and would be shot dead. (Sometimes, fuckers would just run them over for fun as well.)

The patrol lasted eight hours, and we were back in camp by first light. It was hard but, looking back, it was a good show of force to the enemy. We often did foot patrols at day and night, but nothing on this scale with so many guys on the ground at once. It would make things very hard for the enemy to conduct their operations in the future, as they would not know whether or not we would be just around the corner in such force. After this, patrols were stepped up to have guys on the ground at different times, not setting a pattern of life and making it harder for our enemy.

My rotation ended on night patrols before my leave (RNR). I did my final patrol then handed my ammunition in to my Section Commander. I was due to leave for the airport that afternoon with a few others in a convoy, so I still had ammunition for the journey to the airport, but the majority of kit had been handed in.

We got to the airport and there were no delays. On taking off, we had to wear our CBA and helmet till we were out of Iraqi air space, but there were no issues and I was on my way home. In all honesty, I didn't feel I wanted to go home. I was on a roll in Iraq, and all I really missed was a few beers.

Chapter 51
RNR (The Start of Things to Come)

We landed at RAF Brize Norton in the early hours, and I remember as soon as I stepped off the plane all I could smell was the fresh air and grass. It was lovely. However, it was freezing.

I had someone waiting to take me back to Kettering. I had been hoping for my mum or dad, but never mind, a lift is a lift. On the way home, I couldn't sleep, and at one point I saw a wire going across the road and I shouted, "Stop the fucking car!" The car pulled over and I got out in auto pilot; I was looking for a command wire on a UK road. They asked, "What are you doing?" Then I realised where I was and just said, "I'm sorry, needed a piss." I got back in the car and carried on, but I just couldn't switch off.

I spent most of RNR seeing family and friends and getting drunk. Even though I had a young daughter, I just couldn't feel a connection. As bad as that sounds, I was only 20 years old and had been at war for four months, with lots going on.

The Saturday before I was due to fly back to Iraq on the Tuesday, I went out with my friends in Kettering. It started off well in the afternoon, heading towards a night session. It was me with a few lads and a few girls, just having a few drinks. After a few hours, I noticed a guy staring at us from over at the bar, so I asked if anyone knew him. Sure enough, he was an ex-boyfriend of one of the girls, and he had a child with her.

Anyway, when he left then came back, I stepped up and said to him, "Who the fuck are you? Fuck off!" However, one of my friends also had a problem with him, so they both decided to go and have a square go outside, one-on-one, in the middle of the afternoon on a Saturday. So, they went out and had a fight over this young girl.

My friend Ady was losing, but it was a fair fight until the other guy (Mr J) began to strangle him on the floor. Ady started to pass out, so I intervened and kicked J in the mouth and told him he had proved his point, now to fuck off! Then the police arrived – late as per usual. My mate Ady was a bit embarrassed about having his arse handed to him in front of everyone, so he went for it again in front of the police and was arrested. The guy J, who had been fighting with Ady, had seemed to just wander off. So, that left me, Miss C (the girl all the shit was over), a lad called Jamie, and his girlfriend.

We went elsewhere, but someone I knew turned up. She couldn't bear me having a night out without her, even though we had split up!

I soon ditched 'the nightmare', and we moved on to different pubs. But at one point I noticed the nutter J who had been fighting, watching us in an alley. Miss C had told me he was very dangerous and to be careful, so I went over to him and told him I was in no mood for his shit and to leave us alone. I even informed a copper on the beat, but he just replied, "I can do nothing, as he has not broken the law."

We carried on to the local nightclub, where I seemed to stay with Miss C, and we were getting to know each other. After a couple of hours, I noticed the nutter was stalking us from across the club. He had come in on his own and was just watching us.

He came towards me, pointing his long arms and fingers at me, and I blacked out. The next thing I knew I was on top of him, covered in his blood. Miss C told me I had crouched down, hit him in the side, then put a glass into the side of his head, cutting his ear off. Once again, as I say, I blacked out and had been fighting for my life.

Miss C and I went into the female toilets, where she cleaned me up. Then we tried to get me out of the club unnoticed, walking normally, holding hands as if we were a couple. But as we got outside, the fucker was in an ambulance and pointed me out, so I was arrested straight away.

I really didn't think it was that serious until I was charged with Section 18 GBH the next day, which can carry a sentence of up to 15 years in prison. It was not good news for me, but I had to go back to Iraq so I would just have to deal with it when I got home. I still had 6-8 weeks of war to get through.

I felt I had let myself down, but I didn't expect the shit I got in on RNR to follow me back to Iraq. Yet it did… with certain people.

Chapter 52
Back to Iraq after RNR

I was back in Iraq after two eventful weeks on RNR, and now on bail. When we arrived at the airport in Basra, it was explained to us that the IED threat had gone up, and there was now the EFP in town. It had disabled a Challenger 2 tank and destroyed Warriors, killing four soldiers. So, there was now no movement on the MSR without armoured support.

Luckily, there was a convoy going to the Shatt, so I hitched a lift. When I got back, though, it seemed that every fucker already knew my business. I was straight in front of the OC and CSM to explain what had happened back home. I said it was self-defence and that I had just hit out with a glass in my hand. They were not too bothered, but the Sergeant from the Mortar platoon that I shared a room with gave me a really hard time over it, as if I had glassed his wife or daughter. It was fuck all to do with him, so I couldn't understand his problem. But his attitude started to affect my performance and attitude, and I began answering back and arguing with NCOs.

Nevertheless, life went on and I still had a job to do. So, I carried on with the rotations and tried to control my anger.

IDF Attacks

It was more dangerous outside the wire now, and there was more incoming IDF. Our accommodation, as I think I mentioned, was not hard cover – just mobile huts with air con and beds fitted. So, the Company decided to build blast walls in between all the mobiles, in the event of a mortar or rocket round landing within our living area. At the time it was a pain in the arse, but looking back it was a very good shout.

One evening, I had been on day patrols, and it was my shout to get the pizzas in for the room. I was making my way back to the room, walking in the open past the boat yard overlooking Cigar Island, and I was about 30 metres from the accommodation when there was a loud bang. The next thing I remember is walking around with the pizza while the area had been mine taped off towards my accommodation.

I was in a bit of a daze, my ears ringing, and not really understanding what had happened. And when I got back to the room, the pizza was cold and in a mess, with the toppings everywhere. It became apparent that a mortar had landed and exploded in camp, as well as an unexploded mortar – hence the mine tape.

Everyone had assumed I was in hard cover in the main building, but actually I had been out in the open. I can only assume I was knocked out cold by the explosion or fell, hitting my head due to the blast, as I have no recollection of anything else. I just told everyone I had been in hard cover, and apologised for the pizza being cold and in a mess.

I did have a few cuts on my head and hands, and I felt like I had been hit on the head by a hammer, with an awful headache and my ears ringing like fuck. It was a very strange situation. In all honesty, I have no fucking idea what happened. But never mind, I'm here telling the story.

Black Sunday Basra Riots

5 Platoon was on night patrols, but everyone had been wakened and stood to, because a situation had arisen in the city, outside a police station. Two SAS soldiers had been arrested, dressed as Arabs, and negotiations had begun to try and get them released. The Iraqi police were having none of it, and 3 Company were already on the scene with members of the Staffordshire Regiment with their Warriors, using their armour.

As the situation started to escalate with pissed-off civilians, 2 Company was also dispatched with full riot gear, and of course weapons and ammo. The crowd became violent, throwing petrol bombs at the troops. One petrol bomb landed inside a Warrior turret, setting the driver from the Staffordshire Regiment on fire, and as he got out, covered in flames, he was bombarded with rocks and petrol bombs. (I remember seeing this on Sky News after it happened!) The crowd was out of control, and at some point lethal shots were used against those who were putting human life in danger.

The riot went on all day, and we had guys going down not just as casualties from hostile activity, but with heat stroke and dehydration. The police were refusing to realise the two guys were SAS troopers and that their lives were at risk. The boys don't mess around, though, and in the end they drove a Warrior straight through the wall of the police station, doing what they do best – killing the bad guys and getting their boys back safely.

While all this was going on, 2 and 3 Company, as well as the Staffordshire Regiment in their Warriors, were on the base line, taking all the shit from the locals throwing petrol bombs, bricks, and anything they could get their hands on. There was also the occasional small arms fire coming from unknown locations. Due to the chaos, it was not possible to identify a firing point – just pot shots coming, I presume, from windows of nearby buildings.

The lad who was in one of the Stafford's open turrets did manage to escape while they were under attack, but he was alight like a bonfire. Thankfully, he did survive, but with injuries.

Once we had word that the SAS had their guys, it was time for extraction, but the militants had also had time to get themselves into locations ready to ambush us on the way out. We had a guy from the Parachute Regiment attached to us – a Colour Sergeant – and when we got comms that it was time to extract, he deployed a smoke screen so we could get the fuck out of Dodge and mount the vehicles. In the heat of the battle, he pulled out a smoke grenade and threw it into the crowd. But, by mistake, it was a Foss smoke grenade.

All the troops hit the deck to take cover, but none of our guys were hurt by the grenade and everybody made an extraction back to any military vehicles that were in sight, even though some were damaged. Once everyone had been accounted for, the extraction was made, though we came under random RPG and small arms fire from roof tops and windows.

Once back and the Re Org had been done, it became obvious that we had some 3 Company guys at the Shatt, while some 2 Company lads had ended up at OSB, due to the confusion during the extraction. We did sustain some battlefield casualties, but thankfully – due to the professionalism of all troops concerned – all were minor and could be dealt with by a medic. In the circumstances, it could have been a lot worse. The casualty rate of the rioters and militants was unknown.

Everybody was fucked, but we had to stay in control. I was then attached to the CSM multiple as top cover, and went out that same night to drop off the 3 Company lads and pick up our 2 Company lads. We also wanted to show force, but everything was quiet. Apart from a few horrors cutting around at this point, we were on high alert and ready to fight. We just hoped the fuckers wanted to fight fair for once!

The threat after this went through the roof. All the hearts and minds work we had done appeared to have been for nothing, and many of the locals turned on us. So, we were prepared for a difficult six weeks to two months left of our tour.

From then on, we went out in full force and used a hard approach. We looked more aggressive wearing helmets, and appeared harder and more ruthless with the uncooperative civilian population. On every patrol after this we had to be even more observant and totally professional. IEDs were being found all over the place, and we had more IDF on the Shatt al-Arab, as did 3 Company at a base known as Old State Buildings.

Night Patrol

It was three nights after the riots, and the whole area was extremely hostile. 5 Platoon was tasked to go to SLB, with Warrior support, to pick up a new draft (new soldier), then link up with a big convoy including Challenger 2 tanks for a joint operation all around Al Basra, named OP Cardel. This operation involved escorting the Royal Logistics Corps going round all bases in Basra and resupplying them with ammunition, food, water, NAAFI stock, and essential items. This was done regularly, but usually just as a small joint operation. However, due to the hostility and how big the threat was after the riot, it was decided to go in force. We were also briefed that the local militants were looking to kidnap soldiers in retaliation for the damage caused by the riot.

We did a few drops then went to SLB around 10.30pm, picked up the draft who was in my snatch, then hooked up with the rest of the convoy. It must have been at least a 30-vehicle convoy, with snatches, Warriors, Challenger 2 tanks, and the RLC in the middle with their supplies.

20B was at the rear of the convoy, my snatch was the last one, and behind us was a Warrior. So, we set off on the convoy and I was on top cover with Mr M. We visited a few camps, then began driving down the main MSR – the best known route for IED or ambush attacks. As we were driving, I could hear our snatch making strange noises, so I informed the driver G through PRR. He said he already knew, and as the snatch started to break down, G pulled over. I was trying to communicate with the Warrior and our other snatch of 20B, which included our Platoon Sergeant. But when we came to a halt, the Warrior passed us. The chances are that it didn't see us. It was a dark night, and with all the vehicles in the convoy, all you could see was sand.

At first, we sat in the snatch. I was trying to reach someone with the PRR, and we had a Corporal trying to use the Bowman radio, but nothing seemed to work. I was still on top cover, and watched the convoy carry on until it was out of sight. G was trying to start the snatch, but it was having none of it.

This was a time to pull together and work as a team. There was only half a multiple of us (as seen in picture), so we expected that the others would notice we were missing at an RV and come and recover us. Leaving the new guy on top cover, we got out of the snatch and did five- and 20-metre checks, well aware that we were in an extremely dangerous situation. We only had our personal weapons, with a fair bit of ammo, but this didn't include a GMPG or LMG.

Although I was only a GDSM, I suggested we set up a VCP and make out as though we were meant to be there. This was agreed, so Mac and I began stopping traffic and just speaking the little Arabic we knew, like "hello". While we conducted the VCP, G had his head in the engine, but he had no idea what was wrong with it. He was an infantry soldier, not a mechanic!

We were there for a good hour, and I noticed a car I had already stopped had approached again. After searching the occupants again, I waved them off. I then said to the CPL and the team that I thought we might have trouble, and we agreed that if that car came back, we would need to take action. We waited another half hour or so, then I saw lights from a vehicle, so I used signals to make it stop.

It was the same fucking car – three times it had passed us – so I went into combat mode, putting my made-ready rifle, with UGL loaded, through the window and put the barrel to the driver's head. I shouted to Mac, "GET THAT PRICK OUT AND SEARCH HIM!" So, Mac got the other Arab out of the car. I was very forceful with both of them and had one of our guys search their car while I had my sights firmly on the two Arabs, who had been searched and cuffed with plastic cuffs. We found a weapon, but also paperwork.

I am not saying I totally took charge, as we had a CPL, but I was the only one coming up with ideas. I dragged the Arabs off the road and suggested that we take the ECM out, man pack it, blow up the snatch with HE and FOSS, steal the car we had just stopped, and leave the driver and his friend tied up on the side of the road. Everyone at first agreed, and we started to pile into the car before blowing the snatch. Then the Corporal started saying we couldn't take their car. I said, "WHY THE FUCK NOT? WE ARE IN SERIOUS SHIT, G!" But he was too scared to steal the car, so this meant un-tying the two Arabs and letting them go.

I said, "Now we are in shit. We need to tab off and deny the snatch." So, we all agreed to man pack the ECM and head towards SLB, which was a good 18 kilometres away. But it was straight down the MSR, and seemed to be a prov-en route, as it's the way we had come. I wanted to blow up the snatch with an HE to stop the militants getting hold of it and using it to their advantage, or setting it up with explosives. But again, I was told we would just lock it up. I believe to this day that every decision made by the Corporal was wrong, but I was not going to go against what he said to that extent. I didn't fancy a court-martial as well as a Crown Court case!

So, we tabbed off in the direction of SLB, with no commu-nication with anyone but ourselves, limited water and medical supplies, taking it in turns to carry all the heavy ECM. I was still concerned about the guys we had pulled out of the car. If they were militants, they would be looking for us; if they were not, they would have probably gone to the Iraqi police and reported the incident, which meant we would be wanted men and they would shoot first. We patrolled on either side of the road tactically, all of us using night vision.

As we patrolled past a building on our right-hand side, there were armed guys on the roof. We kept calm and I shouted, "As-salamu Alaikum" ("Peace be with you", in Arabic), and gave them a friendly wave. We passed them and got about 100 metres beyond the building, when suddenly rapid gunfire went off in our direction. We all peeled off to the left of the road, getting into all-round defence, linking legs as we'd been taught in training. The tracer rounds were going over our heads and seemed more like warning shots, as the tracers were high but still in our direction. We held back from firing because at this point the last thing we wanted was a fire fight with only half a multiple (less than eight men), no Comms, limited medical supplies and ammunition, and carrying ECM. If one of us was hit, he would have died, that's for sure. We only carried enough trauma kit to keep a casualty alive till he reached a hospital, and that was not going to happen with no Comms. There could also have been fuck knows how many of them there, so the odds would not have been in our favour.

We all peeled off, one after another, giving each other cover while moving into the desert, where we took cover in the sand and had a rest and a chat before deciding what the fuck was next.

We had a drink of water and decided to patrol towards SLB through the deep desert sand, as it was getting fucking dangerous on the MSR. It was around 3-4am, and we could see the lights of SLB in the distance, but we had another problem. Before getting to SLB, we would have to pass an Iraqi-manned checkpoint (PVCP).

We had a Re Org and a discussion before getting in sight of it. We didn't know whether to just tab casually to the checkpoint, try to avoid it, or tactically go past it. The big issue was that they might have been tipped off that there were armed guys walking around, stopping cars, forcing the fuckers out, going to steal their car then apologising, letting them go then being contacted down the same road! We decided to tactically head towards the checkpoint using our night vision and military tactics Charlie and Delta fire teams with limited men. We moved, took cover, then the other moved, passing us, taking cover (pepper potting). The checkpoint had a sanger on the top of it, but we couldn't see anyone manning it.

We got closer and closer till we were under the sanger, then gave cover for the rest of the fire team to make it under the sanger, keeping zero noise. We then tactically made our way round the sanger. The main building had one Iraqi police officer sleeping with his feet up on the desk. Mac and I went to check the sanger and there was an Iraqi police officer asleep on the floor.

Communicating on PRR, we made the decision to take both prisoners by waking them up. Mac and I would do the lazy sleeping beauty in the sanger, the others taking the overweight guy sleeping in the office. So, we woke them both up. Mac and I took the guy from the sanger to the office in the building and cuffed them both with plastic cuffs. By this point we were all tired and pissed off, so the plan was to steal the police car and drive the last three or four kilometres to SLB. This time we all agreed. The sun was coming up and it had been a long fucking night. So, we tied up the policemen and looked for the car keys. Throughout all this, we had guys outside giving cover.

Just as we found the keys, one of our lads shouted, "There is a multiple coming to the checkpoint."

It was a multiple from 1 Royal Irish on a routine morning patrol. They didn't have a clue who we were or what had happened, so when we explained to the Commander, he could not believe it. Their interpreter apologised to the police for us, and we then mounted the Royal Irish snatches. We then drove all the way back to our snatch, which was amazingly still there. We approached with concern, as it could well have been rigged with booby traps, but surprisingly it had not been touched at all. It was safely recovered and driven back to SLB along with us.

When we got to SLB, we waited outside an office where a Commanding Officer of 1 Royal Irish came and saw us. The first thing he did was shake our hands and congratulate us. He got his map out of the AOR and we explained to him where we had broken down and then where we had been picked up. I told the CO, "Sir, I pulled over a car that had approached us three times at the VCP. I wanted to steal it and drive back."

The CO replied, "Well, that would have been a better idea. It's amazing you are all still in one piece and alive, going all that way. That area is for armoured vehicles and convoys, NO foot patrols." Then he laughed. We also told him about the contact in which we'd peeled off into the desert then tabbed through the sand. We explained step by step what we had done, including tactically moving towards the Iraq VCP, finding them asleep and taking over, and admitted we had been going to steal their car until we saw the morning patrol.

The CO then said, "Lads, well done. You have acted in an extremely professional manner. If you were my boys, I would be very proud and recommend you for something, as you have gone above and beyond the call of duty, and we do not expect or train for this in any way. But that's up to your Battalion. We have let them know you are here. They didn't sound very happy!" Later in life, I met former soldier and author Andy McNab for a documentary and told him about the incident, and he also agreed with the CO from 1 Royal Irish.

We were shown to a tent where we got our heads down, as we were fucked. But that afternoon, our Platoon Sergeant came into the tent shouting, "GET UP, YOU SHITS, AND

GET IN THE FUCKING SNATCH!" I could not believe he would talk to us like that after the night we had just endured.

Once we were back at the Shatt, our CSM said, "Right, you're back. Then none of this is to be spoken of ever again, do you understand?"

"Yes, sir."

He then said, "I mean it. Anyone gobs off about this and you will be fucked off out of here and to 7 Company (the ceremonial company in London). It never happened."

I felt really fucking cheated. I had already had one recommendation taken off me because of my actions on RNR, and now we had just gone beyond the call of duty and apparently it never happened! We never even got a well done, and most of the company didn't know about it.

I asked my friend L ,who was in the other snatch in our multiple, and he said they didn't even realise we were missing till they got to OSB early in the morning. They had come under heavy IDF attack, and it wasn't till the Re Org to go back to the Shatt that they realised we were missing. So basically, we were out all night with no communication to anyone, in great danger of getting contacted, and no-one had even known we were missing. I then realised why we had been told to keep quiet. If we had got a recommendation for this, the Battalion would have had to admit there had been a serious fuck-up. But that wasn't our fault.

My attitude really started to change towards the NCOs even more so after this, and I wanted out of the Company. I was pulled into the office by the CSM for having an attitude, so I just laid my cards on the table. I mentioned my recommendation for both the promotion course and for a mention in dispatches being stripped because I done something outside of work. And I also said that it was bullshit we had to keep quiet about our night patrol, explaining that the CO of 1 Royal Irish had said if we were soldiers in his Company he would be a very proud CO and write us all up for a recommendation of some kind. (I was stood to attention through all this.)

He went mad, shouting and swearing, but I just let it go over my head. When he was finished his hissy fit, he said, "Fuck off out of my sight!"

I asked for permission to speak before leaving, and he said, "Go on."

I said, "Sir, I don't care any more if you kick me out 2 Company. Can I go to Support company?"

"Get out of my office" was the response!

For the next week I was sanger-bashing (on guard), eight hours on, eight hours off. I knew it was out of pure spite from the CSM because I'd had the audacity to speak up and ask the questions that should not have needed to have been asked.

During this time on guard, there were a lot more IED strikes. With the new EFP IED on the scene, the Battalion could form covert sniper and recce teams to go out and set up observation posts (Ops) at known vulnerable points, try to catch the fuckers in the act, and kill them.

I was selected by the CSM from the Sniper platoon to be put in one of these teams as rear protection for the Sniper/Recce team. I was really happy to take up this role, as I knew I would be good at it. I also felt a massive weight lifted off my shoulders, as I would no longer be under the command of 2 Company for the remaining five weeks of the tour.

Attachment to Sniper and Recce

I was put in a four-man team. Altogether, we had four teams, and each team had a handpicked soldier from a rifle company for rear protection. I felt honoured to be part of this, as I already said.

Before I deployed, I had to sit in a brief with all members of the teams involved. The CSM asked, "Which one of you is the guy who shot the reporter from Sanger 3?"

When I put my hand up, he said, "Well done, good job. More of the same if we need rear protection, ok? No bullshit from us guys in this platoon, and first name terms. Ok, Ben?"

"Of course, sir," was my reply, and I got a wink in response.

In the brief, we were told that basically we would be going out at night to known locations near where IEDs had been laid, also to IDF positions, and to set up observation posts (OPs). The operation was different every night, and sometimes we would be in the OP for anything from 12 hours up to 48 hours. We didn't just go to known areas that had been attacked; we also went to other vulnerable points (VPs) and set up OP there. I was excited after this brief, as it was just the sort of soldiering that got me going.

After the brief I had to go and see my new Sergeant, whose team I was in. He explained our new SOPs and issued us with equipment like infrared glow sticks, which you can only see with night vision. We were also given more night vision.

We all went out on the ground and did our own covert operations, and sometimes worked together covering Multiple VPs, with each team in a different OP.

We always deployed under the cover of darkness – sometimes on foot out of the front or rear gate, other times we would go in a snatch that was on a routine patrol. When the snatches stopped and the troops did their five- and 20-metre checks, we would take cover, wait for them to leave, then once everything was quiet, we would get up and move to our RV point for our relevant operations. We also got to use the Commando-attached boat platoon where we would deploy from the rear of the Shatt on a military speedboat (manned by a team of Commandoes), be tactically dropped off at a location, then we would get in all-round defence till the boat left us. We would then make our way to our relevant RV point. Sometimes the selected OP on the map was no good, therefore we would have to find elsewhere to set up an OP.

Depending on the operation, we would sometimes be deployed wearing a mix of green and desert uniform, other times just deserts. If setting up OP in an area with grass or moving on foot covertly, we would often apply CAM cream, taking into consideration the state of the moon. We used the saying Shape, Shine, Shadow, Silhouette, as we did not want to give our position away. We only used 1x ECM, which was the lighter one, as this did not have such a high frequency and did not piss the dogs off as much when we were trying to move tactically and undetected.

I was attached to this team for roughly five or six weeks. Some operations were very hard, with long tabbing for hours before setting up an OP before sunrise. Sometimes we would deploy for 48 hours, so would be carrying enough rations and water for the task. At points it was very tiring, and often boring, and when you are tired at night and haven't slept properly, you tend to see things that are not there.

When tabbing, we would set up RV points all the way to the objective (OP), so that we knew where to fall back to in the event of a contact or if we got separated. Before getting to our selected OP, we would always stop short, get in all-round defence, and assess the situation before the Recce team member made his decision on the best route for him to lead the team. This is when we would be at our most vulnerable, because these routes had all been selected due to recent enemy activity. For all we knew, there could have been an IED already there, so we had to clear the whole area without using any sort of white light (as this would give our position away). We used our LLMs (night vision, as I previously said) to clear the area, then moved into position to set up the OP.

Most of these patrols were uneventful, so possibly the local militants had been tipped off. However, there were a few interesting incidents.

One night we were tasked to deploy by boat to the other side of the island – we were on the boundary of Iraq and Iran – then to covertly make our way towards the Shatt, setting up snap Ops along the way, and keeping an eye on known hotspots and enemy activity locations. Then at the FRV, we had to set up an observation post overlooking the island in the middle of Shatt al-Arab River, which we called Cigar Island. On this operation we went green and desert, and wore camouflage cream.

We had to be on the ball with timings, because the locals would be up at 0400 with the speakers screaming out in Arabic so that they could go to the Mosque to pray. We needed to avoid this time or it would completely compromise our task, not to mention be fucking dangerous in that area.

On one particular task, we had no choice but to move through a small village. We got there around 0300 hours and tactically moved through the village, keeping out of the light. Suddenly I noticed a woman lying on the side of the road. I was suspicious, so called a halt to the team on PRR, then we all went firm and got into cover and fire positions. I approached the woman from the rear, as it was the safest way, and could smell a hell of a stench (not unusual in an Iraqi village).

With my weapon pointing at her, I nudged her with my foot, then the barrel of my rifle. She was clearly dead, but I then wondered if she had an IED hidden inside her (this was a tactic they used on dead animals). We were in an unfriendly village that troops rarely went through, so the chance of her being rigged was slim. However, if we were discovered to be patrolling around, the chances of a full-on contact were high.

I took a step over her head to see her face, and it was clear she had been dead for some time and had just been lying there rotting away. We had wasted five minutes with this, so had to move on and leave the corpse. We didn't realise how big the village was, and just before we could exit the village, we noticed people getting up ready for prayer time. We had to lie low straight away in any place that offered cover in the dark, keeping down while the speakers were screaming out in Arabic, calling for prayer. We stayed in cover, keeping our breath and movements as still as possible. The ECM was turned off in case a dog heard the frequency and went mad, which would have compromised us. We had people walking past just five feet in front of us with no idea we were there. It wasn't till we couldn't see anyone moving around that we knew they were either in the mosque praying, or in their homes. We used this time to get out of the village, passing the mosque where I remember seeing lots of flip-flops outside.

Anyway, we managed to get out of the village without being seen, and made our way to our FRV point, then to our OP. Keeping our eyes on the objective, we made it before first light, and we then got into routine, waiting to see if the insurgents would show up! The next morning, we cleaned all cam cream off our faces and changed into full deserts, changed from our CWS night sights to our regular SWSAT sights for daytime use, then we tabbed as if we were a regular patrol back to the Shatt al-Arab Hotel. This time we took a longer route, passing through another small village and using a different way back just in case we had been spotted and there were any surprises waiting for us. We got back without any issues after what had been a tough night, but one that had been successfully executed.

Another operation that was eventful saw us deployed by snatch with a routine rifle company patrol. When they stopped to do a VCP, we dismounted into the desert two kilometres from our OP, which was at a VP where there had been recent sightings of suspicious vehicles coming and going. It was also a VP that had previously been used for IED strikes.

We tabbed in at around 2000 hours as usual, using RV points along the way, and this time in full deserts. We had to occupy an old war-torn building. As usual, we stopped short before the Recce team member decided the best way in, with us all clearing the way as we entered the building. Then we found the best cover to set up the OP on the objective, and got into routine. We staged on all night and were due to stay there till noon the next day, keeping eyes out for possible enemy, before tabbing back to the Shatt roughly three kilometres away. We always had a designated area to take a piss, and if you needed to have a shit then we carried bin bags, because we could not leave behind any evidence that we had been at any OP. That meant all rubbish and empty ration bags had to be taken with us as well.

The sun was up, we had a good all-round defence, and there was nothing in sight, so I informed the Sergeant I was going to take a piss. I went to the designated piss area at the rear, but as I was just finishing, I spotted a blue car coming from the rear through a dirt track, not a road. I dropped to the floor behind a rock with my weapon ready, my combats covered in piss, as the car stopped and the two occupants got out.

My Sergeant said quietly to me via PRR, "There are two people right in front of you. We have you covered, just stay there and keep quiet."

I could hear the two guys waffling shit for a few minutes, then they got back in their car and drove off. Our sniper team could not shoot them, because there was no evidence that they were militants, but the car and plate were logged and reported up the chain of command. We were all sure they had been there to do a Recce to plant an IED, the fuckers, but unfortunately it wasn't enough to engage them. And if we had apprehended them, it would have meant compromising our OP, so unfortunately all we could do was log down the details of the car and the two pax that were there. This information was fed up the chain of command and logged, so it wasn't a bad result when it came down to intelligence. To this day I can't believe how close I was to them, once again getting away from what could have been a life-threatening situation. That being said, I had cover from an elite sniper team, so the biggest problem was the lingering smell in my direction of bad breath, cigarettes, BO, and cheap aftershave!

A few other OPS were going out at night, covering troops doing foot patrols in the day. We would deploy at night, set up an OP, and provide over-watch for the troops on the ground, making sure no-one was setting up any unwanted surprises for our boys. We were also keeping eyes on possible and previously known sniper positions.

While I was deployed on another task with the specialised platoon providing cover for ground troops, my rifle platoon (5 Platoon) were on patrol in the daytime. They dismounted at a VP and did five- and 20-metre checks before walking the snatches through the VP. One of the lads at the front noticed some foam, took a closer look, and saw it was some sort of IED. However it was an EFP, so an immediate halt was called, they reversed out of the danger area, and EOD went in to deal with the device. It turned out that it was what we called a daisy chain device, which means that as soon as you set off the first device, there were more IEDs attached, making a hell of a noise and a mess. Had that soldier not noticed the foam and taken one step more, the device would have set off the daisy chain and would have definitely killed some, if not all, of the section.

I deployed on task with the team on a 48-hour OP looking for the bad guys setting these EFPS/IEDS. The next afternoon, we arrived back at the Shatt to be told we were leaving and moving back to SLB that day, and that our replacements had arrived. I'd had no idea, because I had been deployed with the snipers and recce specialised section. And although I was still living with 2 Company, I didn't see much of them; when they were in, I was asleep, and when they were asleep, I was out on tasks.

So, I packed my gear, handed in my ammunition and specialised kit, leaving two magazines with rifle as we still needed to get to SLB. Then we were airlifted from the Shatt by helicopter.

We were all looking forward to seeing 3 Company, who were apparently due to meet us at SLB. But we got to SLB to find there was a very negative vibe. We were all called by the RSM, where he sadly informed us that a Sergeant H had that afternoon been on his last patrol of his six-month tour, doing a familiarisation patrol with the new Battalion, when he had been hit by an EFP and sadly pronounced dead at the scene (KIA). He was a married man with children. Even now, I can't imagine or want to imagine the pain his poor family must have felt getting this news just 24 hours before he was due to return home. This was a massive downer and loss for the Battalion at the end of what had been a successful tour, not to mention the loss for his family.

We spent a few days at SLB before going to Basra Airport, where we flew home to the UK.

Chapter 53
Mind-Changers

I will never forget the strong smell of grass both times I landed from Iraq... particularly the first time. It was amazing.

But looking back at my time there, some little things that stick in my memory are certain incidents that happened that maybe shouldn't have. Like a water bottle being thrown for kids and ending up in the Shatt River. There were some US Dollars in the bottle, and two young local boys began fighting for it even though there was a note inside for both of them. Kids would always fight when you threw them a bottle of water or some USD, and to be honest we would just let them get on with it. If that's how they wanted to act, it was up to them.

However, on that occasion only one boy came out with the bottle; I assume the other must have drowned, as the current was very strong and the water very deep. Of course, none of this was intended, and efforts were made to find the boy, but to my knowledge he wasn't found.

Towards the end of the tour, the locals began to become very hostile, throwing bricks and rocks at us. We couldn't open fire at people throwing rocks, but we could use flares, aimed above them so they caused no injury. Even though we were met with hostility, we still had to remain professional. The mad thing was that at one point in a certain area they wanted to be your friend, then the next they would be throwing rocks at you. However, if the pattern of life was completely different and there was no-one around, usually it meant we should prepare for a contact. So, it was a good combat indicator.

The number of dogs that were killed being run over by vehicles as well as being shot bothers me. I won't mention names, but a tortoise was also found on a patrol, picked up, and I watched someone hit it several times with a shovel to see how long it would last till the shell broke and the poor thing died. At the time, you have to laugh about it, but I'm an animal lover and now I would like to do that to the guy's head. Maybe it's those actions in Iraq that have made me such an animal lover to this day, but I would rather take a human life than a domestic or wild animal any day!

During one patrol, I had gone firm by the side of my snatch when I saw a child come out of an alley roughly one metre or less in front of me, holding an AK47. I wasn't made ready, only loaded, so I quickly made the dash to the young boy and disarmed him, breaking his arm in the process. The snap was too loud to ignore, and the AK dropped to the floor as he ran off crying. His angry father came to his aid, weapons were raised, and we mounted our snatches and fucked off. It turned out that his AK hadn't been real; in fact, it was made of fucking plastic. The boy was lucky to only suffer a broken arm. If he had been 15, 20 metres away, pointing that at us, I would have dropped him, regardless of his age or gender. If I had known it was plastic, I would have done nothing, but in those situations you can't take that chance.

During my time on Op Telic, there are also things that happened that to this day I cannot and will not talk about, and the only people who know are my best friend (my wife), close family members, and a couple of close friends. It's not just me, but others have to deal with these things as well for the rest of their lives, and I certainly cannot talk about it in a book. But before people cast judgement, they need to be there to experience these situations first-hand.

In a nutshell, I'm very proud to have served in Iraq with my Battalion's battle group. I also have no regrets about anything whatsoever; force is met with force, and kindness with kindness. We were an elite fighting force battle group, and we executed every task with the utmost professionalism, including hard knocks, counter terrorism, and dominating the ground down to hearts and minds.

However, the tour I was on in 2005 took and injured the lives of more soldiers and contractors than any tour since the Iraq invasion to that date! We all had a very busy time especially in downtown Basra, which also saw the rise of the so-called Islamic State, ISIS.

Chapter 54
Is This Reality?
(Life Back at Home)

After landing back in the UK in the early hours of a frosty October morning, we had to unload our baggage and load it onto a truck, then we were driven to Lille Barracks in Aldershot. When we arrived, we saw that some flowers had been laid outside the camp for the two soldiers we had lost.

That first day was as if we had just got back from an exercise in Salisbury Plain. First, there was a Muster parade to make sure we were all there, then we had a day of moving back into our relevant accommodation, checking serial number kit and cleaning weapons, then having them inspected before handing them into the Armoury.

Once everything was complete, which took two days, we were stood down for a long weekend. We had no welcome home or victory parade whatsoever; it was just as if we had come off some bullshit exercise in the UK. After the long weekend, we had a week of work to do, getting things back to normal with all the usual bullshit, then we would have our post-tour leave, which was three weeks' long.

We did, however, have a 2 Company party in Guilford, which turned out to be a major piss-up and led to loads of us going on to a club. It all kicked off that night inside the club and continued outside. There were people knocked out on the floor – some of our guys, and some of those we had been fighting. I had given a lad a good kicking when I saw him kicking my mate while he was down. I left him in a mess and was trying to bug out, as I could hear police sirens.

I hid in one of our lads' cars (we called him Stretch, as he was nearly seven foot). We put the seats down, and I hid under loads of coats and whatever shit he had in his boot. Outside, I could hear the police asking about the lad who was in a mess, and looking for who had done it. Luckily, I got away with that one.

The next day, on morning parade, most people had black eyes. A few had been arrested, and I believe one was in the medical centre. No-one knew about the state of the others we had been fighting, but thankfully no charges were brought for anyone. It was just one of those nights! Men will be men.

I finally got to do another driving course, which I passed in three days, as I had been driving for years and had a BMW at home. However, drinking and driving was something I was doing a lot, and eventually I got caught. I was banned for one year and given a £1500 fine, as well as yet another promotion ban in the Army.

However, it didn't stop me, and I actually smashed up a number of cars over the years. I was lucky to only slightly injure myself and my cars, with one exception, when I seriously smashed up a BMW on a motorway at extremely high speed. Luckily for me I have friends willing to help me out in good places. However, I didn't get away Scot free, because in some of the smash-ups I had, I was seriously injured but had to go back to camp, say nothing, and carry on with training. I must have written off three cars in a year.

In the motorway incident, I was on leave at the time. I broke my ribs, had whiplash, and looking back have no idea how I didn't die. I was lucky, fucking stupid, and not proud of it. But the biggest upset for me was that being banned from driving put me on a 12-month promotion ban in the

Army – in my eyes that was the real punishment. I received my licence back after 12 months and didn't need to retake a test; the DVLA just sent me a new licence with the endorsements on it.

I was drinking much more and was finding life at home very difficult, but I did not want to show any sort of emotion or weakness. I was having nightmares, constantly thinking people were out to get me, and this led to me getting in lots of bother both at home and back in the Battalion.

My family were always telling me I had changed and they thought I had problems, but I just ignored them. One of the things that really pissed me off was the NCOs who did not deploy on Telic, like the Regimental Police Sergeant (I won't mention his name, because he is a wanker). He was so bitter and twisted and would go out his way to make life shit for the lower ranking members of the Battalion, checking their boots were polished at 1700 at dinner time, or reporting them if they did not have their MOD 90 ID card in their top pocket – just totally unnecessary bullshit. He pushed one GDSM too far one day. I'm not sure what he said or did, but the GDSM went into his office with a plank of wood and smashed his head in with it.

I was struggling to cope with normal day-to-day life, and back in Battalion I felt as though there was a dark cloud over me due to the remarks I had made back in Iraq about our patrol that got left behind. Then there was the drink driving ban, not to mention the GBH charge I was facing from when I had been on RnR. I was having what felt like constant daydreams about Sanger 3, the night patrol when we were on our own, and other incidents we had been involved in. But at the time I thought this was all normal. In fact, I just wanted to be back in Iraq, not in the UK tossing it off. This was clearly the start of PTSD, but I just didn't know it; I didn't even know what PTSD was.

When I visited Kettering Magistrates for the first hearing of my GBH case, I did not know the severity of a Section 18.

I was in court for less than an hour then bailed for the case to be transferred to Northampton Crown Court. I was also put on Pub Watch and barred from all pubs in Kettering. Every pub had my picture behind the bar, as well as on the CCTV monitors. I know this because my friend was a security guard and always gave me the heads up.

As life continued, I was not adapting at all, and I was getting into all sorts of trouble both at work and home. I couldn't sleep, my attention span was zero, I was paranoid and having flashbacks all the time. All I wanted to do was go back to war or drink myself stupid. There were still certain pubs that overlooked my ban, so I stuck to them. I even shaved my head to change my appearance, but that fooled no-one!

Night Out in Leicester

One night, along with two mates (both named Lee) who had also just got back from Iraq, I went out for the evening in Leicester. One of my friends also brought his little brother, who was 16. We were having a good night until we went on to a club. After about an hour, an argument started between our group and another one, but somehow it quickly calmed down. I went upstairs for a piss, and when walking back down the stairs, I saw it all kick off between the two groups, so of course I ran down to help out my mates.

As the fight moved outside, I saw Mr M (Lee's little brother) pissing with blood from his neck and getting a good kicking. I ran over and got stuck in, dropping two of his assailants out cold. My friend and I dealt with the last one together, and luckily there was no CCTV down the alleyway.

I then got Mr M out of the way, but the blood was spraying out of his neck, and he collapsed. I picked him up, got him to safety, and looked at his wound. His throat had been slit. I was covered in his blood and took off my shirt, putting it into his wound along with my hand to try to stabilise the bleeding, but the knife had hit a main artery in his neck. I held his hand with my arm around his head, while my other hand was inside his neck.

I managed to slow the bleeding from the neck, but he was coughing blood through his mouth and was dying slowly in my arms. His brother was next to me, rubbing his head, in tears, while the other Lee was pushing people back who wanted to see what was going on. Mr M's dad had passed away a few years before, and I remember as the young lad's pulse was slowing down and he was drifting off, he said, "I can see Dad, Lee. I am going to see Dad."

He was dying and needed urgent surgery. And even though 999 had been called, it seemed to take ages for the emergency services to arrive. In fact, two coppers were the first to arrive. One tried to take over from me even though I had Mr M stable and he had a slight pulse. I got very aggressive with the police officer and refused to let go of Mr M until a paramedic turned up. Eventually the ambulance arrived, and he was rushed to hospital with his brother. One of the paramedics told me, "If he survives, you saved his life."

The other Lee and I were left standing on the street. I was topless, my body covered in A's blood. About 20 minutes after the incident, the police turned up in their meat wagons, and Lee and I were arrested. We had no idea why.

At the police station, we had all our clothes taken off us for forensic evidence, even though it was clearly Mr M's blood on me! We were given paper suits and led to the cells. I was told that Mr M's condition was critical, and that this could be a murder investigation. They had also arrested the other group who had been fighting with us, and incredibly one of their lads was in our regiment, from 3 Company. (He got a separate slap from me a few months later.)

I was interviewed later the next day and told that Mr M had survived and was now stable, but he had needed a blood transfusion and 80 staples. However, because I was already on bail for a separate incident, I was deemed to be a suspect – even though it was me who had saved the lad's life. The investigation was led by CID, so we were all bailed pending further investigation, and given grey tracksuits to wear.

When I got back to Battalion, things didn't look great. I was on bail again for an investigation into a violent disorder and attempted murder charge. This time, though, I felt totally innocent, as everything had been purely self-defence and two other guys would back me up – one of whom was facing the same charges. However, it made life difficult for me because it meant there were now going to be two Crown Court appearances.

I felt my time in 2 Company was over, so I volunteered to be put on the 81mm Mortar Course and become a Mortar Man, starting again in Support Company. My application was accepted, so I left 2 Company and was put on the Numbers Course (Mortar Course).

Chapter 55
Joining the
Mortar Platoon

I joined the Mortar Platoon a few months before we were due to move to Windsor. We completed a difficult course that consisted of training through the day and night, lots of PT with extra weight (as Mortar kit is fucking heavy), and lots of dry exercises with the drill mortar, until we were good enough to pass as a number 1, 2, and 3. The course itself was two weeks in-house training, then a two-week exercise at the end, followed by a live firing exercise in the UK with HE/Smoke/and Illume. After this we were badged as Mortar men. However, the training never stopped, and we would always be on the ranges doing live firing or, if in camp, PT every morning, followed by training after.

We also kept on top of our Infantry skills as a rifleman. But every night that we had spare, we would be on the piss till the early hours, then hanging out our arses on PT the next morning. As long as you kept up, it was all good, but if you fell behind, you would get a hell of a beasting. We all tried not to fall behind, but when you are out on the piss till 6am and have a run at 0800, it can be a struggle. However, it was even worse if PT was at 1500, as by that time the hangover had well and truly kicked in!

As I said, joining the Mortar Platoon meant more training and responsibility, which also earned respect. However, this meant heavier nights out on the piss. Some nights we would get in and go straight into the junior NCOs' mess to carry on, as my friend was in charge of it and he loved a party. Sometimes during a working week we would be up drinking till breakfast time, then have scoff, a shit, shower, and shave, and be on parade for roll call.

One Wednesday evening, we all went out to Maidenhead and had a great night, getting back at around 2am. After signing in (in the guard room), I sneaked through a window, and with my mate watching out, I went into the kitchen of the guard room to nick some night scoff, rolls, crisps, etc. When I got out, I heard some girls outside camp.

I looked at my mate and said, "Come on, let's bring them in." Next thing I knew I was on the floor. And when I stood up, there was blood running down my head. I had run straight into a steel post outside the guard room, and the scoff I had stolen had fallen out of my pockets. It was quite funny really.

I tried to walk back to my room, but my good friend and medic woke up and took me to the med centre and fixed me up. The next morning, I had forgotten about what happened till I looked in the mirror and saw the big scar down the middle of my head. I still have that scar today. I wish I could say it's a war wound, but it's not.

I re-joined the Battalion boxing team, but with so much going on, the Company wouldn't let me progress as I wanted.

My GBH case was coming on quickly, and I was still on bail for the other incident in Leicester. I went to visit my solicitor and barrister to discuss the evidence, and he told me, "Ben, I am sorry, but you could well be looking at a prison sentence of up to three years." I felt sick and went all weak for a few seconds. We had a chat about options, and I left feeling very down, with a lot of documents the barrister had given me.

The paperwork was over 200 pages long, but I sat and read through everything. I also had access to the victim's criminal record, and the number of times he had been to prison and charged was ridiculous. He had even been sent down for sexual assault. But none of this mattered in my case.

While I went through the paperwork, I noticed that the police had made a huge mistake. While blanking out certain bits of information, they must have used a pencil or something to scribble out his full name and address, because I could clearly see it, so I knew his full name and address. I also still knew his ex, Miss C, and was seeing her in my spare time.

I was on duty when I had a call from the solicitor to say, "Ben, the victim has withdrawn his statement, and the CPS are dropping all charges!" I had got away with it and was in the clear for this one. Only the one in Leicester was hanging over me now, and as far as I was concerned, I'd acted the hero that night for saving A's life.

It was a massive weight off my shoulders to be cleared for the GBH charge, but I was still struggling to sleep and to fit into normal life in Battalion and at home. I was drinking too much and still becoming very aggressive with people. I would also keep looking at people of a certain race on the train or walking around town, thinking that they were a threat.

During this time of struggling to cope, I bought a BMW. One day I went to visit my friend in Huntingdon, and decided to drive home at night. But while driving home, I blacked out and I thought I was back in Iraq on top cover driving down the MSR. Before I knew it, I had crashed into the central reservation of the motorway, destroying the car, and seriously hurting myself – though I did not feel anything till the next day. I left the car, concussed, not realising how far away from home I was, and just kept walking down the A14. I tried knocking on parked lorries, but no-one was answering.

At one point, I saw a sign that I was still 15 miles from Kettering, and by then the pain was starting to kick in and I began to panic. I walked to a farm where I lied and said I'd had an argument with my wife and had got out of the car. I asked the farmer if he could please order me a taxi to Kettering, but the pain started to kick in even more, and the next thing I remember was him waking me up on the ground. I had collapsed in his doorway. The guy was so kind and drove me back to Kettering himself, refusing to take any money from me. I got him to drop me off a few streets away from mine.

When I got home, I had to explain what had happened, and literally an hour or so later the police were knocking at my front door, having obviously traced the crashed car back to my address. I took full responsibility, my car was recovered, and I incurred all the charges. The next day I went to A&E, and while waiting I saw two police officers with a prisoner in handcuffs. I thought, *Fuck this,* and left hospital before being seen. I'm not sure why, as the police were aware I was just in an awful state of mind.

It took me over a month to fully recover from the crash, and you would think I would have learned my lesson. But I was a ticking time bomb, and my mind was seriously playing tricks on me. Looking back, I was very poorly mentally, but I just didn't know it or want to admit that I needed help.

Chapter 56
Move to Windsor
(Royal Duties)

We moved to Windsor to Victoria Barracks, and what a shithole it was compared to Lille Barracks in Aldershot. It's a very old camp, located about 300 metres from the Royal Windsor Castle. The main problem was moving from new accommodation at Lille Barracks, which consisted of single-man rooms for support company with an ensuite bathroom, to Victoria Barracks which looks basically like a prison. It has a big 20-foot wall all the way round it, with razor wire on the top – funnily enough, facing in the way to stop people getting out – and CCTV on every corner. There were two gates, and if we had used the gate at the back, we would have been entitled to London pay, which was roughly £150 extra per month. But because we used the main gate at the front, it came under a Slough postcode, so we were not entitled to London pay. What a load of shit, the Army conning their own troops!

Inside Vicky Barracks was horrible as well. It was a rectangle-shaped, three-storey building for all lads who ranked under a sergeant; basically three levels of long corridors separated by doors for relevant Platoons and Companies. The accommodation was also not good; it was mostly small four-man rooms with shower rooms down the corridor, like being back in basic training.

The only good thing about Windsor was the fact that the camp was only two minutes from the pubs and nightclub. I did not like Windsor, though. I was struggling enough without all the bullshit that went with royal duties as well as all the tactical exercises. It was like being back in training. I did not feel like I belonged in the UK, and I wanted to be back in a hostile environment, so I kept putting my name down for tours with other battalions when they came up. The problem was that as a new member of the Mortar Platoon, I was needed at Battalion.

When the Battalion announced that it would be holding an intercompany boxing event, straight away I got involved. I was fighting for Support Company and Mortar platoon. All boxers were meant to be struck off duties, company PT, and normal training for at least a month to train, but this was not the case for me and a few others from Support Company. I had two sparring sessions before the competition, and was made to do Monks March the week before the first fight.

Monks March

The boxers from other companies were exempt from this. (Not me, or the rest of Support Company lads, though.) Monks March was a 40K Tab in Cumbria, with teams of four or five having to hit checkpoints, then complete tasks before carrying on. This exercise started on a Tuesday and finished on the Thursday evening. It was hard, and about 70 percent of the people involved did not manage to finish. We had three hours' sleep throughout the whole exercise, and our team finished with three despite starting with five. Even though we were fucked and knew we had definitely not won it, we ran through the final checkpoint and it felt good to finish.

We got back to Battalion for the weekend off, and on the Monday afternoon I was boxing! As it goes, I won the fight by KO in the second round against a guy who had been struck off duty to train. Then I had to fight one day later in the final.

During my pre-fight medical, though, the medical officer failed me to fight because I had a high temperature. I was gutted. I was also made to feel like shit by my Colour Sergeant, as if I had bottled it and backed out the fight. I wanted to fight but the medical officer had refused me, yet apparently this was not good enough and I had let the platoon down! Bullshit!

Chapter 57

Royal Duties, Trooping of the Colour and State Opening of Parliament

To start with, it was a real honour to be a Queen's Guard and do royal duties, but as time went on it just got ridiculous doing 24 hours on then 24 hours off, or sometimes 48 hours on and 24 hours off. Being in Windsor meant being up and ready to leave by 0530, then get to Wellington Barracks to do a full rehearsal in normal combat 95, and once this was finished we might – if we were lucky – have an hour of down time to grab some bits from the NAAFI. At around 1030/1045, we would be in bearskins, tunics, tweeds, and drill boots, and marched onto the drill square where the Change of the Guard would start. Every day I would wish for rain, as that way we would cut out all the bullshit and just march straight to relevant locations, i.e., Buckingham Palace or Saint James' Palace.

The best duty of all of them was the Tower of London, as it meant less bullshit, and you did not have to be involved in the parade. We still performed two-hour guards, protecting the Crown Jewels, and were very close to the public. The guard duties lasted two hours apiece, after which most the lads would just sleep, but I liked to walk around the tower in uniform, getting lots of attention from the public – mostly the ladies.

The only downside was at 2200 hours every night you had to perform a ceremony called Changing of Keys. It's a re-enactment of what happened when the keys were changed over every night when the Tower of London was a prison. Every night there are around 80 to 100 people there to watch this ceremony, and I hear it's very hard to get tickets, with up to a year's waiting list, if not longer. One time while I was at the Tower of London, Prince (now King) Charles turned up to give us a personal inspection – not that he had a clue what he was looking at.

At first, preparing all your ceremonial kit is a total ball ache, but you pick up ways of cutting corners. The best one is using a produce you can buy from the supermarket, called Klear. It's used for polishing floors, but when applied to your drill boots, they shine like mirrors – and it only takes seconds. The only problem is that if it's raining, it can leave a blue-like stain on your boots. However, me and the lads worked out a way to stop this happening by using a black ink cartridge from a fountain pen. When you mixed this with the Klear, it stopped any stains if the boots got wet.

On one inspection before a parade, the CSM said to me, "You have used Klear on those boots, haven't you?"

I replied, "No, sir."

He just looked me in the face. He knew, of course, but it was down to the Duty Officer to do the inspection. When the Officer came to inspect me, he said, "Well done, GDSM. Good order." This meant you would get some sort of privilege.

After the parade, the CSM said to me, "Fair play, if the Officer gives you good order then you got away with it, but you don't fool me. But I will not bag you if the Duty Officer doesn't!"

He was a good CSM. Other times we were not lucky and would have a total wanker who would pick you up for faults, which would mean you pulled an extra duty. It's just a big game really. Usually the Battalion would be undermanned or there were too many people on the sick chit list, which meant no royal duties. So, I think they were looking for excuses to bag you so that they could fill a spot for another guard.

We also had the pleasure of doing Barrack Guard at Victoria Barracks, and also the Royal Castle of Windsor. Windsor was the best out of the royal duties as it was only a five-minute march up the road and did not start till 11am, so there was no rushing about.

I was on the rear post at the Royal Castle of Windsor, facing out into the garden, when the Queen was in residence. It was protocol for someone to tell you if a member of the royal family would be coming past so that you could present arms. Well, this never happened one afternoon.

I was stood on guard at ease, when I heard the big doors opening. I stood to attention, not knowing who was about to come out. It was lightly raining, and I first noticed the Corgi dogs, with someone holding up an umbrella and a few other people walking alongside. As the Queen was in residence, it was double tap; this means two guardsmen on either side of the posts. I was the senior GDSM, therefore it was my responsibility to call out all drill commands.

When the group had passed, I looked over at the other GDSM and asked him, "Who the fuck was that?" He just shrugged his shoulders, so I assumed it was no-one important.

After about 20 minutes, I noticed the small group coming back, and I could hear the doors opening from the inside. I gave the order to stand to attention again as they passed, but was still unsure who they were, due to the weather and the umbrella. They walked straight past us and into the castle, then the doors locked, so I ordered us to stand at ease.

A few minutes later, a police officer came to me and said, "Why didn't you present arms to the Queen as she passed you?"

So, it had been the Queen walking her dogs!

I replied, "Why didn't one of you halfwits warn me she was coming out? I'm not fucking psychic, am I? She had an umbrella up, with people around her, and I cannot see through people, can I? You lot are meant to warn me when she is going to pass us, so it's your fault." As it goes, nothing was ever said about it anyway.

I had to do a CFT on the Monday morning, and I was in total agony from another car crash I had caused over the weekend. I'd been a twat as usual, hurting only myself, writing off yet another car, and having to get friends to help me clear the mess from the accident on the Saturday. I could not report sick because I didn't want to make a fuss. but I suppose I deserved every bit of pain I was suffering.

I had a habit of crashing cars when I was pissed. The very first time was outside my house, when I was not shit-faced but definitely over the limit. I skidded on ice and into next door's car, but lucky for me he agreed that we would deal with it in the morning – no police, just insurance.

And all this shit I was getting involved with was raised 80 percent after Iraq!

Chapter 58

Spring Drill

Every year we had a week of spring drill, which is held at the former Guards training depot, and it's basically a week of total bullshit and beasting on the drill square, doing every kind of foot drill to arms drill, as well as guard mounts. It wouldn't be so bad if it wasn't the fact that your kit had to be 100 percent perfect every day, and if you got picked up for anything, you would find yourself on another duty at some point, or a 22-hour show parade at the guard room that night, being inspected by the Duty Officer. Our Battalion loved 22-hour show cleans, and every day someone would get bagged, whether it was spring drills or not. It's almost like it's a game for non-commissioned officers to see how many AGAI 67s they can dish out in one day.

The AGAI 67 was re-introduced into the Army in 2005, and is a document you sign to say you accept the punishment. Of course, if you feel it's totally unjust, you can refuse to sign it and request the matter goes before a court-martial. Sometimes you have to do that, because some NCOs will take a personal dislike to you and use and abuse their rank as a form of bullying, so there are times you need to stand your ground. If you do request it to go to court-martial, it will be thrown out unless it's very serious. And then you can guarantee you will be on the shit list radar.

Trooping of the Colour and State Opening of Parliament

Before we did the Troop and State Opening, there was lots of bullshit to go with it – training every day, doing drill, and being inspected, and of course there was always time for a daily PT session.

I was involved in two Trooping of the Colour and State Opening of Parliament. I had the job of street lining then mounting guard after, at either Buckingham Palace or St. James's Palace. Of the two, St. James was the better location, in my opinion.

When we were street lining, you had a week of practice beforehand on the Battalion drill square, in full drill kit, which had to be perfect even though we were just practising. Before the Troop or State Opening, we'd have an early morning full rehearsal in London during the night/early morning, so that everyone knew their position for the next day and what was expected of them.

On the day itself, we would deploy to Chelsea or Wellington Barracks, prepare our kit, and get ready for a long day ahead. The point of street lining is stopping the public from reaching the Royal Family when they pass down the long road. You can be standing there for up to five hours or so, and if it's a red-hot day (which it usually is on the Troop) there are always a few people who collapse. One particular time a GDSM collapsed, and his bayonet went through his neck. Luckily, apart from a scar, he was ok.

We do change positions with the GDSM on the other side of the track at times, when the Duty Officer or Sergeant shouts the command, so this keeps the blood flowing through your body. The CSM or SNCO will also regularly march down the lines, adjusting your bearskin and slipping a sweet in your mouth to suck on; if you're really lucky, a sip of water. When the Colours pass your position, you change drill movement to slope arms On the Command (we have plenty of time, as it's passed down the line). When the Royal Family pass, the Order to Present Arms is called, and you can be standing at that position for as long as five minutes or more. If it's a State Opening of Parliament, you have to wait for the Royal Family to pass again on their way back to the Palace, and go through the same procedure. When it's all over, we march off in companies to our relevant barracks or, if you are unlucky, to one of the palaces to mount guard duty.

After one of my Troops, we were back at Windsor and on the beer straight away. I was barred from Chicago's for fighting, and as it was a Saturday I thought, *Fuck it, I will go home to Kettering*. I picked up eight cans of beer and made my way home. I was shit-faced and fell asleep on the last train, only to be wakened up by the train conductor.

I asked him, "Mate, where the fuck am I?"

He replied, "Derby, mate."

I could not believe it, and my phone had died. I got off the train and asked a member of staff when the next train to Kettering was. She said, "7am."

It was bloody midnight, and all I had was my clothes and two cans of beer. I walked into the town, not having a clue where the fuck I was going, but I found a nightclub so went in there on my own. As I was standing at the bar, I heard someone shout my name and noticed a guy who I had met on my driving course, who was in a different regiment. So, I hung around with him and his wife till I met a local woman at the end of the night. It was about 3am when the club shut, so I found a hotel for the night then made my way back to Windsor the next day. (What a night!)

So anyway, life went on, doing back-to-back Guards PT with not much time off in-between, because in the time off we had we would be preparing our kit for the next guard mount. Somehow, though, we always found time to go out for a session. In fact, every time I was on duty at St. James's Palace at night, we did not do guard, just QRF. So, I would change into civvy clothes, then go out in London for a bite to eat and, of course, a few cheeky pints.

I kept volunteering for overseas exercises and tours with other units, as well as courses, but what was holding me back was my promotion ban. However, I finally got lucky me when me and my friend Lee (also on bail for the attack in Leicester) volunteered to make up a Multiple of Coldstream Guards for a winter tour of Bosnia.

We both struck gold and were accepted to deploy in late November 2006. We got struck off duties to do some in-house OP TAG training with our respective Multiple Platoon Commander, and SGT and team. We had to complete our basic military tests, i.e. fitness, along with the APWT (shooting test), to get a tick in the box to say we were deployable.

We were only deploying for three months, but I could not wait. Even though it was only low-level peacekeeping operations, it still meant I would be on tour!

Chapter 59

Bosnia

2006/2007

It was the night before we deployed to Bosnia. Our coach was due to leave for the RAF airport at 0430, and as Lee and I had already packed, we went out on the piss and got totally shit-faced. I took some local girl back to camp (she knew the way better than me, lol!), and we only had about two hours left, but that gave me enough time to do what was needed! As I got into my uniform, she asked, "Why are you getting ready?"

I said, "I'm off to Bosnia, girl, in 30 minutes!"

I got her to carry my kit down the stairs for a laugh, as I knew that all the lads going on tour would see us. They laughed and cheered as I got on the coach to drive to RAF Brize Norton.

Lee and I were still totally shit-faced, but we had plenty of time to sleep it off while we flew to Bosnia by Hercules C130. It was fucking noisy, but we put our ear defenders on, got out our sleeping bags, and slept.

When we arrived at Banja Luka (Bosnia), it was freezing, as you would expect over there in the winter. We were picked up and taken to the metal factory, which was an international military base, and attached to a different regiment.

On the first day, we were shown our accommodation and I was sharing with an NCO called Mr M, who was also in the Guards regiment who deployed with us. He was the guy I had defeated in the second round of the boxing tournament earlier that year, but that was sport, not personal.

We all had a drug test by urine, then had some cold weather kit issued, and sent off to do PT. The PTI was a total bellend and started bagging us for the type of trainers we had on, as they were not military issue Hi Techs. We all did a BPFA and some other fitness tests, but the PTI was just abusing his rank and trying to act tough.

The next morning, we sat Briefs and were updated on current threat and what to expect over the next three months. It was not a dry camp, which meant we could drink alcohol, and there were two bars where the lower ranks could drink, with last orders usually at 11pm, or midnight on a Saturday. It would be fair to say that me and a few others were in there every night we could, getting plastered, then hanging out our arses the next day as per SOP! There were plenty of females in the metal factory, so one night I got lucky and was smuggled into the female accommodation.

There was also a place you could go and eat. It was nice, had Wi-Fi, and was like a pizza shop but also offered snacks. Only soft drinks were served in there, though. We had a big mess hall, but it was shit Army food, as you would expect, so the pizza place got lots of business. There were no cash machines in camp, so we had to go to the main admin office and sign for money which they would then deduct from your month's salary.

Bosnia was not what I had expected at all. Yes, we were on tour and did some low-level operations, but it seemed more like a training depot, with all the companies competing to be the best. Every morning we did PT, and it was tough PT. We would also be up in the mountains doing Arctic warfare, which was good training, but at temperatures as low as -30C, it was fucking freezing.

One day on an exercise up in the mountains, we were doing live section attacks in the snow, and a Halt was called. One of the Welsh Guardsmen had spotted an anti-personnel mine from the war. So, we had to evacuate the area quickly but carefully.

We sat lots of mine briefs and were taught how to search for mines using a rod, and the best way to evacuate if we ever ended up in a minefield. On the map of our area of responsibility, the red dots indicated known fields which were places to avoid. We would frequently deploy out to these known areas, keeping to the safe tracks to make sure no-one was in the field. Unfortunately, during this tour, a farmer was killed by a mine while he was chasing one of his sheep through a field.

While there, I was involved in the international tug-of-war competition. Our team finished runners-up in the final, beaten by a team who I think were Dutch and clearly on the juice (steroids). But runners-up out of roughly 15 teams was good going.

Christmas Day, 2006

On Christmas Eve, we were stood down from work unless on duty (Guard), and luckily I was not on that night. Every member of the lower ranks was in the bar that evening, called the Foundry, and we all got totally shit-faced and had a good party. Early the next morning, we were wakened with GUN FIRE (this is coffee with lots of rum in it) by the Platoon Commanders, CSM, and SNCO, and they also gave us each a Christmas box to open that contained items like a can of deodorant, sweets, chocolate – silly things just to boost morale. Most of us had cans of beer we had smuggled out of the bar the night before, so we just got straight back on the drink.

Christmas lunch was to be served at 12.30 in the mess hall, and we all marched there, half pissed, where food was served to us by the CO, officers RSM, CSMs, and SNCOs of all the Welsh Guard Companies.

It was a three-course meal, and every table had a couple of crates of beer and cider on the table. Before the main course, the Commanding Officer made a speech and wished us all Merry Christmas. Then we all got tucked into our main course, with the banter from all companies intensifying and getting louder and louder. After the dessert had been served by the officers, the Regimental Sergeant Major, with his loud drill voice, told us to quiet down so he could speak. He wished us a Merry Christmas and warned us not to get too drunk or to cause any fights between ourselves! A pissed soldier shouted, "Aw, fuck off!" Then a big food fight started between us all in the mess hall. (It's a SOP to have a food fight after Christmas Dinner in the Guards.)

Later that night there was a party in a big tent, set up with a DJ and makeshift bar, from 7pm till midnight. We kept drinking and had a good party, with only a few scraps with people, but that's just how it goes. Most of us were more interested in the females that were stationed at our camp, and there were a few!

New Year's Eve, 2006

New Year's Eve, I was not so lucky, and neither was my friend Lee. We were given a task and deployed on QRF, to set up an OP high up in the hills, monitoring the camp and surrounding areas. It lasted all night and was shit, but at least we'd had a good Christmas. You have to take the good times with the bad, and do your part. Being in the military isn't a complete party. "Train hard, fight easy."

January 2007

International Tactical Military Assault Course Competition

Even though I was a pisshead and fucked about a lot, when it came to military skills and tactics in the field, I was second to none. And that is why I was selected to be part of a tactical assault course. It went on for miles and, being January in

Bosnia, the ground was covered in snow and ice. It involved overcoming obstacles put in our way, as you would expect on an assault course, but this one also included live firing with all types of weapon systems. There were weapons I had never used before, such as the RPK machine gun and a Sniper Rifle not used by the British Army, as well as the SA80 assault rifle, GPMG machine gun, and Javelin anti-tank weapon (this was an electronic one).

There was a hidden tank in the distance that we had to find, and also drill mortar already set up. So, we had to apply the C2 sight and lay onto a target given to us, then use drill rounds to destroy the target. There was also a British Sniper rifle shoot, where once again we had to find the target and take it down. All these shoots were spaced out along the assault course, so by the time you had got to a firing point, you were blowing out your arse. The targets were also not clear, which meant we first had to identify them, then fire. There was a safety officer at every shoot who would give us our instructions, then we would get on with the task with as many rounds as we had been allocated.

There were also boring tasks where you had a couple of minutes to set up a radio and send a Sit Rep of your location. And as the course was carried out in the mountains in the snow, it was freezing, and we had to crawl through slush and run through ice water. By the end, we were fucked, but it was a great experience.

The course lasted all day, and it was timed. There were also points for hitting your targets. Only one team could go through at a time, due to the live firing throughout the course.

I was paired with my Section Commander for this, and although we did not win, we completed the course and destroyed all our targets. Out of about 50 teams, we finished in the top ten. As some teams did not even complete the course, I felt a personal pride to have been selected for this and to have successfully completed the challenge.

Boxing Team in Bosnia

The regiment I was attached to announced that they would be holding an inter-company boxing competition in six weeks, and was looking for fighters. Me and a corporal were the only two from our regiment who volunteered, so we would be fighting for 2 Company (The Jam Boys). Our trainer was the Quartermaster of 2 Company, and we trained every morning at 0630, then again at 18.30, Monday to Friday. This meant we were struck off company PT but had to do all other training.

Boxing was good, and I felt better and faster than I had previously. Unfortunately, all the hard boxing came to a halt after three weeks because 2 Company were deployed to Sarajevo for a week to do Public Order training (Riot Training), as there was a heightened risk of some public order out on the ground. We still got some pad work in on an evening, but it was not the same as good training in the ring.

Sarajevo (Bosnia)

The Public Order training saw us act as rioters as well as defending troops. Every soldier loves a bit of Public Order training, as it gives you a chance to let out some aggression.

When we were acting as rioters, it was against the Italian forces who were deployed there. They used their normal riot gear of metal batons and six-foot shields. So, when they advanced, we withdrew, because no way would you stand a chance with head, hands, and feet, against a platoon in full riot gear. We just kept a safe distance, throwing petrol bombs, bricks, and any other missiles we could find. It was a great laugh.

We had our own exercise to do, though, and it was tough riot training. The reason for this was that intelligence suggested the local population could start a riot over the smallest thing, so we had to be ready to intervene.

On our final exercise, I was at the front of the base line (I was used to public order from Iraq) and we were going from street to street, clearing, while having petrol bombs and missiles of all kinds thrown from 'the rioters'.

A petrol bomb is always thrown with an element of safety in training, as it's only to simulate the real thing. However, one petrol bomb was thrown in my direction, and it hit a rock, flipped up in the air, and somehow dropped on my side of my shield and ignited. I tried to stamp it out, as per SOPs, but the flames were spreading up my combats, and I could not breathe due to the carbon monoxide from the petrol. I could see the flames coming under my visor.

I dropped and rolled in the snow for what felt like hours, but was really only a few minutes, then someone put me out with a fire extinguisher. My adrenalin was pumping, so I got back up and carried on with the exercise. It was not till after the adrenalin had gone that I realised what had happened, and that all my clothes were burned to a crisp. I was virtually naked.

I was asked if I was ok and replied, "Of course." But that was for show.

Later that night, I could not stop thinking about it, and still do today, especially when the flames came up under my visor and I couldn't breathe. If it had been a second or two later, the flames would have been exposed to my bare skin and I would probably have suffered first degree burns. As it happened, I did not have a scratch on me except that my eyebrows had been singed.

Back to the Metal Factory

We moved back to Banja Luka after our week away, and there were only two weeks till fight night, so every day was spent on boxing. I had to fight the other NCO from my regiment, and I severely broke his nose in the second round, winning by a knockout.

I was fighting in the final, and it was a few days before I found out who my opponent was. After watching him train, I was extremely confident that I was going to beat him, but I was so over-confident that I took it easier with training and had a session on the beer a few days before fight night.

On the night before the weigh-in, I was two pounds too heavy, so I could not eat, and the next day I was in the gym on the treadmill, running for two hours in a hat, jumper, and long trousers, trying to sweat it out. When it came to the final weigh-in, I made the weight, but I felt ever so weak.

I was one of the last to fight and only had a small platoon of supporters out of about 1000 spectators, as they were all Guards or attachments. I was in the blue corner, and when my music came down, I felt good but still slightly weak after training all day to reduce my weight. Unfortunately, I was still far too confident, and in the first round my opponent got a good shot on me in my left rib, cracking it. I carried on fighting, but by the end of round one, for some reason I felt totally fucked – probably due to being over-confident and drinking a few days before the fight.

The second round was fairly even, as was the third. Even though I had a bad rib, I felt I had won that round, as I kept my rib protected and let him advance to me, jabbing him, and landing a few rights after moving from his punches.

The bell ended and the fight was over, and it went to the score cards. He got the decision on points.

I was pissed off with myself, as I knew I could have easily beaten him if I hadn't let down my guard with my final days of training and being too confident. And it taught me a lesson not to take things for granted. That night, all the boxers went to the SGT mess and got hammered on free beer. I actually asked the guy for a rematch, but he declined.

While in Bosnia, Lee and I had to call our solicitor about the incident in Leicester that had almost cost young Mr M his life. We were both told that all charges against us had been dropped and that only the other group were being charged with GBH, except the weasel we knew from our regiment. But at least he had already received a slap as punishment.

This was really good news for us both. The guy who stabbed Mr M was sentenced to three years in prison; the others, I think, six months apiece. What pissed me off was that the press reported that a police officer and paramedic had saved Mr M's life, and classed everyone involved as thugs, when it was actually me who saved his life.

I did not have much time left in Bosnia after boxing for three weeks or so, and I was not looking forward to going back to Windsor. Our Platoon Commander had said that when we returned there, we would be on leave for ten days as we had been deployed over Christmas. So, at least that was some good news.

We all left Bosnia better and fitter soldiers, because it had been pretty much three months of training. I, however, was determined to try and make the Army boxing team, and my Platoon Commander told me he was recommending that I should be put on a JNCO course. The decision was not down to him, as he was a Rifle Platoon Commander, but he wrote me a glowing after-tour report. Before we left the multiple, we were awarded our operational medals – my second.

Back to Windsor 2007

When we got back to Victoria barracks, it was early morning midweek. Lee and I were expecting to go on leave the next day, so could not believe that our names were down for a royal duty the following morning! For a start, we did not even have our kit.

At 07.30, we went and spoke to the Mortar Platoon Sergeant, who then spoke to the CSM while we both stood in combats outside his office. At 0800 he called us both in together and asked us what the problem was. It was as though we had just come off an exercise for a week. (It was reminiscent of 2005 in Iraq.) Anyway, he made a phone call to Battalion HQ, who confirmed we had been granted leave by the Commanding Officer from that day. So, we were stood down for ten days, and both went home.

Knowing that I was going to receive a glowing report from the course, as well as no further action from court, I was quite excited to get back to Battalion for once.

However, I was in for a shock. While Lee and I had been deployed to Bosnia, the rest of the Mortar Platoon had been to South Africa on a month's exercise. Our Sergeant seemed to take this personally, and said, "So, you wankers are back after medal hunting, are you?" He treated us like total shit, as if we had been traitors, and not one word was said about my good report. I even asked the Platoon Commander we'd been with in Bosnia if he had given the report to my platoon, and he had. So, I felt very let down once again.

I was still very much into boxing and was training in my local boxing gym when on leave. On return, I approached the Battalion PTI and expressed my interest in trying out for the Army boxing team. He was very positive, but told me he would have to first check with my Platoon and Battalion.

Within 24 hours I was back in the Platoon office in front of my Sergeant, getting a major bollocking. "You fuck off with a rifle company on tour, come back, then want to try for the Army boxing team!" he said. "Do you want out of my platoon?"

I replied, "No, sir. I am just trying to make the best out of my Army career. Did you not read my report from Bosnia, and my recommendation for the promotion course? I thought you would be pleased, sir."

He said, "Pleased? You are a fucking Mortar man, not a Rifle man, and you will go on promotion courses when I decide. Now get out of my office!"

I left feeling like shit and as if all my hard work had been a waste of time. It seemed that my ambition to get into the Army boxing team was not going to happen, so life went on as normal – training, PT, and more training, with back-to-back guards, and field exercise.

Once again with a complete lack of support, I felt I was on my own. I was drinking too much and messing around, trying to hide my mental health problems. I would go out and drink every night of the week, whether it was with the lads or on my own. And insomnia was getting the better of me. I drank to get to sleep, but I was also drinking to hide my emotions. I was angry when I drank, and I was angry when I was sober. The problem in these situations is that no-one speaks out and shit rolls downhill, so the cycle repeats every day! It was like I was stuck on a never-ending hamster wheel.

My head was fucked, my life was a mess, and I was questioning everything.

Had I fulfilled my promise to my grandad of becoming a soldier, or had my brain created a nightmare that could ruin the rest of my life?

Had the war started at home as a child, or followed me home from Iraq?

To be continued…

Glossary

ARCS - Arcs of observation & Fire
ACF - Army Cadet Force
APWT - Shooting Test
AOR - Area of Responsibility
BAT SIMULATOR - Virtual training for flight.
BFT - Basic Fitness Test
BFPA - Basic Personal Fitness Assessment
CWS - Containerized Weapon System
CFO - Combat Fighting Order
CBA - Combat Body Armour
CFT - Combat Fitness Test
Civ Pop Training - Riot Training
CSM & OC - Company Commander
EFPS - Explosively Formed Penetrator
EFP - Explosively Formed Projectile
ECM - Electronic Counter Measures
EOD - Explosive Ordnance Disposal
EX - Military Exercise
FRV - Final Rendezvous point
FIBUA - Fighting in a Built-up Area
GBH - Grievous Bodily Harm
GPMG - General Purpose Machine Gun
GDSM - Guardsman
ITC - Infantry Training Centre
IEDS - Improvised Explosive Devices
IDF - Indirect Fire Alarms
IDF Alarms - Horns to warn of explosives
IRTC - Infantry Training Centre
IED VBIED - Suicide Bomber Threat
JNCO - Junior Non-commissioned Officer

LSW - Light Support Weapon
KIA - Killed in Action
LECs - Locally Employed Civilians
LLM - Light Laser Monocle
LAW - Anti-tank Weapon
MFO - Boxes
MSR - Main Supply Route
MOD 90 - Army ID
NCO - Non-commissioned Officer
NBC - Nuclear Biological Chemical
OP - Observation Post
OPTAG - Operational Training
OC - Major / Officer in command
OSB - Old State Buildings
Officer - Platoon Commander
PT - Physical Training
PFT - Personal Fitness Test
PTI - Physical Training Instructor
PRR - Personal Role Radio
POW - Prisoners of War
QRF - Quick Response Force
REME - 118 Recovery Company
Reveille - Wake up
REORG - Reorganisation
REME - Royal Electrical and Mechanical Engineers
RSM - Regimental Sergeant Major
RTR - Return Fire
RNR - Rest and Recuperation
RLC - Royal Logistic Corps
RMP - Royal Military Police
RSOI - Reception Staging Onward Movement and Integration
REECE - Exploring to gain military information
SOP - Standing Operating Procedure
SND - Special Needs Department
SIT REPS - Situation Reports
SA80 - Personal Weapon System
SLB - Shiba Logistic Base

Stags - Sangers with Hesco and sandbags for the troops to keep 24-hour watch

Sanger-Bashing - On Guard

SNCO - Staff Non-commissioned Officers

SUSAT - Sight Unit Small Arms Trilux

TAB - Laded March with Weight and Weapon

Two-Miler APWT - Shooting Test

The Juice - Steroids

VPs - Vulnerable Points

VCP - Vehicle Check Point

Wriggly Tin - Corrugated Metal Tin

Acknowledgements

I would like to thank my publisher Cassandra Welford and my editor Christine McPherson for taking the time to work with me and get the story to you the reader.

About the author

Ben, who lives in Northamptonshire, is an ex-Veteran and military contractor. He is very passionate about helping those who suffer from PTSD. It has taken many years to bring his book to life in the hope that he can raise awareness of the devastating effects of PTSD.

Press

Ben has been featured in a previous book sold in Waterstones as well as on GMTV in 2010 for a documentary regarding therapy on PTSD with Talking to Minds Charity. He has also been featured in The Radio 4 Kill Factor, The Daily Mirror, and a National Japanese newspaper regarding his time in Iraq.

Contact Ben

For more information about 'When War Follows You Home' you can connect with Ben Close or Close Publishing page on Facebook or closepublishing@outlook.com benccgs2517@ yahoo.com

Printed in Great Britain
by Amazon